# Online Money Matrix

The Science of Positive Cash Flow for Online Marketers

**WILLIAM MCCAMMENT**

## Legal Mumbo-Jumbo

None of the information in this book is intended to make you think you will make money instantly or that you'll launch a successful internet marketing career overnight. I've made every attempt to relay good information and genuinely help those who read it; however, even the best attempts can fail, especially if the reader does nothing to help himself/herself. You actually have to do some work in order to be successful. Also, I don't know anything about you personally; you might not be cut out for this type of work and have little or no chance of success. All I can do is point you in the right direction and hope you "get it." Also, please be advised that following any of the links within this book could ultimately result in compensation for the author.

Copyright © 2018 William McCamment

All rights reserved.

ISBN-13: 978-1979839303
ISBN-10: 1979839301

# DEDICATION

To my amazing wife, Rachel, who never stopped believing in me... even long after I stopped believing in myself; and my daughter Emily, who's very existence continues to brighten every moment of my life.

# DEDICATION

# CONTENTS

Introduction .................................................................................... 1

ONLINE MONEY MATRIX ........................................................... 9

Getting Rich The Easy Way ..................................................... 11

The BIG SECRET The Gurus Aren't Telling You About Making Money Online ........................................................................... 16

The Missing Element ............................................................... 20

    The Crazy Reason People Aren't Giving You Money ......... 21

Speeding Up Your Success ..................................................... 24

    Money vs. Time .................................................................. 24

    Guaranteed Success .......................................................... 26

You MUST Do This Or You Will Fail (note: you're not doing this!) ......... 29

    The Lifeblood Of Your Business ......................................... 29

    The Standard Procedure .................................................... 32

    Why Experienced Marketers Tend To Pee Their Pants Over This Advice ........................................................................ 34

    Your Primary Mission ......................................................... 37

Affiliate Marketing Isn't A Viable Business Model Unless… ....... 39

    Why You're Not Making Money ......................................... 41

    Using Redirects .................................................................. 42

Creating A Lead Magnet For Affiliate Marketing .................................. 47

Offering Bonuses ............................................................................. 50

Time To Break Out The Calculator ............................................................ 52

How To Calculate Percentages ............................................................ 53


ESSENTIAL MARKETING MATHEMATICS ................................................. 55

Ten Calculations Every Marketer Needs To Know ................................. 57

1. CONTRIBUTION TO OVERHEAD ....................................................... 59

2. BREAK EVEN POINT ........................................................................ 62

3. CONVERSION RATE ........................................................................ 65

4. RETURN ON INVESTMENT .............................................................. 67

5. PROSPECT ACQUISITION COST ....................................................... 70

6. CUSTOMER ACQUISITION COST ..................................................... 72

7. COST PER LEAD .............................................................................. 73

8. VISITOR VALUE .............................................................................. 75

9. CUSTOMER VALUE ........................................................................ 78

10. CUSTOMER LIFETIME VALUE ....................................................... 81


PREDICTABLE MONTHLY INCOME ......................................................... 87

The Plan For Monthly Income ................................................................ 89

How To Formulate Your Plan For Positive Cash Flow ......................... 90

Pro-Level Product Creation ...................................................................... 94

    How To Work With An Outsourcer ....................................................... 94

    Doing It Yourself ............................................................................... 96

    Creating Videos And Audios ............................................................... 97

    Guru Trick To Instantly Increase Perceived Value ............................... 97

    Take It To An Even Higher Level ......................................................... 99

Instant Credibility ................................................................................. 101

    Promise Me You Won't Freak Out… .................................................. 102

    Working Without A Net .................................................................... 102

    The Power Of Live Webinars ............................................................ 105

    The Live Coaching Option ................................................................ 106

    The Live Coaching Gambit ............................................................... 107

    For The Brave With Experience… ..................................................... 109

    Group Coaching .............................................................................. 110

Getting Things Done ............................................................................ 112

    Releasing Into The Wild ................................................................... 115


RADIOACTIVE SEEDS ............................................................................. 117

Important Notes About The Bonus Section ........................................... 119

Welcome to The "Make Money Online" niche ....................................... 122

The World's Worst Online Marketer ..................................................... 124

A Clever Solution To The "Credibility" Problem ............................... 126

Time To Get Serious .................................................................. 128

Why The "Make Money ONline" Niche? .............................................. 130

How to sell to the "Make Money Online" crowd when you've never made any money online .................................................................. 132

Why You Can't Lose With Your First Product ...................................... 135

Pick Something and Go! ............................................................. 136

16 Product Blueprints You Can Use To Start Your Online Marketing Career .................................................................................... 137

Radioactive Seed #1: "X-Ways To..." Report ..................................... 139

Radioactive Seed #2: Summit Report ............................................... 140

Radioactive Seed #3: Fast-Article Writing Course ............................. 142

Radioactive Seed #4: Fast Product Creation Course ......................... 145

Radioactive Seed #5: Reference Guide ............................................ 147

Radioactive Seed #6: Research Pack ............................................... 149

Radioactive Seed #7: Simplified Process Video ................................ 150

Radioactive Seed #8: List of Resources ........................................... 152

Radioactive Seed #9: Interview a Guru ............................................ 153

Radioactive Seed #10: PLR Report .................................................. 155

Radioactive Seed #11: Autoresponder Sequence ............................. 157

Radioactive Seed #12: Marketing Mindset ....................................... 158

Radioactive Seed #13: Software/Web App Instruction ..................... 159

Radioactive Seed #14: Graphics Pack ................................................. 161

Radioactive Seed #15 "What I found out…" Report ......................... 162

Radioactive Seed #16: Video Review Packages ............................... 164

Offering Services .................................................................................. 165

    Article Writing Service ................................................................... 165

    Sales Video Service ........................................................................ 166

Piggybacking ......................................................................................... 167

Doing Your First WSO ........................................................................... 169

    Protected Downloads .................................................................... 170

    Posting Your First WSO .................................................................. 171

Jumpstarting Your WSO ....................................................................... 173

How To Bury Mediocre Reviews And Uncomfortable Questions ......... 176

This is Only The Tip Of The Iceberg ..................................................... 181

Welcome To The Matrix ....................................................................... 183

ABOUT THE AUTHOR ........................................................................... 185

# ACKNOWLEDGMENTS

This book is the result of my more than 20 years of experience in online marketing and sales. But, the knowledge required for that experience didn't just fall from the sky; it came from an almost inexhaustible list of mentors, teachers, entrepreneurs, coaches, associates, family and even customers! So, in order to keep this list to under 50-pages, I'll only list those whose voices continue to ring in my head every day. First and foremost I have to acknowledge my mom, who is the smartest business person I've ever met. Without her advice I'd be nothing. Secondly, my main mentor, Gary C. Halbert. There's rarely a day that goes by that I don't ask myself, "What would Gary do?" Others who have made a tremendous impact on me are (in no particular order): Jay Abraham, John Carlton, Eugene Schwartz, Jason Fladlien, Russell Brunson, Jim Edwards, Paul Myers, Jeff Walker, Eben Pagan, Frank Kern, Travis Sago, Colin Theriot, Joe Polish, Ryan Deiss, Perry Belcher, Todd Brown, Rich Schefren, Don Wilson, Ben Adkins, Sean Mize, Manny Talavera, Tim Castleman and way too many more to list. Finally, I'd like to acknowledge all my friends and family who have stuck by me all these years, but have never gotten a satisfactory answer as to what I do. For those people I can finally say, "Read this book!"

# INTRODUCTION

What Do Successful Online Marketers Know That You Don't?

Are the experts holding back some key information that could change everything for you?

I believe they are, but it's not what you think.

Most successful marketers in the "make money online" niche really do put together trainings that can teach you how to make money.

The problem is, they only show you one or two ways to make money within a specific system.

So you buy their product and implement their system.

Maybe you make money and maybe you don't, but what you really need—the key elements that go beyond just a single system—aren't included.

So you buy another system from a different expert and the same thing happens.

But, these experts aren't purposely holding back some Big Secret; they're delivering exactly what they promised... A specific method for making money.

What they don't do is offer up the science behind it;

the inner workings of their business; the thing that keeps them creating an endless stream of products and making money every single day.

And, that's why I wrote this book.

I want to show you what's really going on.

I want to show you the truth.

But, I have to warn you... It's not for everyone.

The truth is complicated... the truth is difficult... the truth is *messy*...

There's mathematics and blunt honesty involved and it doesn't make for exciting sales copy.

That's why you'll have a hard time finding a pro-level expert willing to share it with you.

But knowing the truth is *absolutely necessary* if you want to break-free of the B.S. and take your online marketing career to the next level.

## Are You Ready For This?

In the 1999 movie, *The Matrix*, Neo, played by Keanu Reeves, is given a choice: He can either swallow the blue pill and remain blind to the invisible truth, or swallow the red pill and see what's really going on.

By reading this book you are, in essence, taking the red pill.

I offer this as a warning because most people, whether they admit it or not, don't really want to see the truth.

Their motivation for learning internet marketing is simply to fool themselves into believing their crappy little lives can be turned into something tolerable.

Knowledge of online marketing methods satisfies a desperate need to believe things will get better; that they won't have to be a slave to a lousy job; that they will one day break free and be in control of their lives.

For these people, hope is enough.

As soon as they believe it's possible to make money online they can tolerate their crappy jobs for one more day because they know there's a way out. They carry hope on their back. Hope satisfies.

When hope starts to fade, they're on the lookout for something new, and the hope-cycle starts all over again.

This spawns what a lot of online marketing enthusiasts call, *Shiny Object Syndrome.*

Shiny Object Syndrome is sort of an online marketing disease that involves collecting ideas to strengthen your dream of success.

Some of these ideas are pretty good and might even work if they were acted upon, but that rarely happens because taking action runs the risk of failure, and clocking-in to a job you hate without hope of a better life would be unbearable.

So, you buy another shiny object to give yourself a fresh injection of hope.

Unfortunately, a lot of digital product creators take advantage of this phenomenon. They produce crappy product after crappy product knowing the majority of buyers will never use the information.

Sure, they get a lot of refund requests, but there's still plenty of profit to keep them going.

I hate these guys because the whole online marketing community becomes jaded and suspects every product to be a potential rip off. They are killing sales for the rest of us who genuinely try to produce valuable information products.

But, I'm not here to get into a rant about shady product creators; I'm here to help you. I want you to succeed in this business and the best way to do that is to open your eyes.

There is no blue pill; I only offer the red one. As Morpheus said in *The Matrix* just before Neo makes his choice, "Remember, all I'm offering is the truth… nothing more."

Open wide and swallow it down. Here we go…

## What You'll Learn

In my original sales material for this book, I included a sub-headline, "Ignore this and fail."

That's really not far from the truth. What I'll show you in this book is mandatory knowledge for everyone serious about a full-time career in online marketing.

I'm going to start out with a few chapters explaining some of the core concepts involved with successful online marketing. You might think you already know all this—and, you might—but, I believe if you really, *really* knew this stuff you wouldn't have time to read about it here. You'd be too busy making money. ☺

I'll also make sure you have a basic understanding of how to use percentages because that's something that will come up quite a bit during the day-to-day operations of a pro-level online marketing business.

I know a lot of you already know how to calculate percentages, but I still think it's a good idea to read that very short section anyway because there are different ways to arrive at the same number and we can all be on the same page when it comes to the precise method I use.

The next thing I'll do is go through some of the hidden calculations the pros use to set-up winning marketing strategies. Some of this will open your eyes to a whole new world of possibilities—the stuff the gurus keep to themselves.

The math won't get too heavy, but you'll definitely need to break out your calculator from time to time. But, don't worry... if you can do basic addition, subtraction, multiplication and division with a calculator you'll do just fine.

After we get the basic marketing mathematics out of the way we'll be ready to put together a monthly strategy for a full-time online marketing business.

I'm even going to explain a lot of the "inside tricks" the pros use when creating successful digital products.

And, of course, much, much more...

What I'm *not* going to do is give you some half-baked money-making scheme that might be working at the moment but will soon be obsolete.

This book will stand the test of time. Most of it will never go out of date because it is filled with universal concepts you'll use over and over again.

Keep it nearby and check back any time you need clarification.


## Bonus Material Added

If you've been around the online marketing scene for a while but, for some reason, you're just not making the kind of money you should (or, even none at all), I've decided to throw in something specifically for you.

It's based on a $27 PDF eBook I created called, *Radioactive Seeds: 16-ways to enter the "make money online" niche with your very first product (even if you've never made a dime online in your life).*

Now, this section isn't for everyone; you may not yet have enough knowledge to create a "Make Money Online" product. Or, you just aren't interested in creating one.

However, I know there are plenty of enthusiastic students of online marketing who could genuinely help other people with the knowledge they already have.

The problem is, these enthusiasts don't yet have any past history or proof of income to back them up; so, they don't feel they have the credibility to produce a legitimate product for the "make money online" crowd.

Radioactive Seeds solves the credibility problem as well as gives you 16-product blueprints that work without having to show proof of income.

In other words, you can create and offer these products for sale without "faking it" or trying to be something you're not.

If this sounds like something you're interested in, you're all set. I've included the bulk of the original PDF in the bonus section. All you have to do is implement the info.

## This Book is the real deal

Another reason I wrote this book is because I'm tired of seeing so many marketers base their businesses on nothing more than convincing you how awesome their products are.

The hype is incredible. I wanted to do something different and offer something that not only tells-it-like-it-is but also delivers real, useful information that every online marketer can use in his or her business every day.

This is critical information and I believe anyone who truly understands the lessons in these pages will benefit for the rest of their online marketing career.

This book shows where the money comes from and where it goes. It allows you to see inner workings that are often invisible to the average online marketer—things that are sometimes counterintuitive and, at times, seem wrong or impossible.

Well, there's a lot to cover, so let's get started.

SECTION ONE

# ONLINE MONEY MATRIX

The science of positive cash flow for online marketers

## GETTING RICH THE EASY WAY

When people come to me wanting to learn online marketing, they very often have the same question: *How can I make a lot of money really fast without having to leave the house or do much work?*

But, as silly as that sounds to those of us who know how much hard work is actually involved, it's not really their fault. They've been lied to.

You can find any number of beautifully written articles and blog posts complete with amazing screenshots of ClickBank or JVZoo accounts documenting how the author has achieved overnight success.

So, people are looking for a magic button they can push and get money without having to build a web site, sell anything, or create a product.

Unfortunately, a lot of "Online Guru" types use this against you. They know if they promise overnight success you'll be more willing to part with your money.

They know the closer they get to convincing you this magic button exists, the closer they'll get to taking your money. They tell you if you just follow their "system" you'll have overnight success too... guaranteed!

But, think about it: If someone was making $5,000-a-day as they claim, why would they give up the secret for $10 (or even $1,000)?

The truth is the gurus really do make lots of money; unfortunately, some of them are making it mostly from selling you their system, not by following the system itself.

If you're one of those who have been duped by this sort of thing, don't lose hope just yet; throughout this book I'm going to show you true, proven ways to make money online.

But, first, we're going to have to start getting real with it.

We're going to have to abandon the thought process that leads too many struggling online marketers down the path of failure.

## Getting Real with Online Marketing

The first concept you'll need to adopt to become a successful online marketer isn't very exciting, but I feel it's important to cut through the crap as soon as possible so we can have smooth sailing the rest of the way. So, here it is:

***Stop chasing instant wealth and overnight success.***

Look... if you need money *right now* there are a lot faster and easier ways to get it than online marketing. Go get a second job or sell everything you can on eBay and Craig's List.

I know that isn't what you want to hear, but looking for a quick way to get yourself out of a financial jam on the internet—especially if you're not already making a predictable online income—is crazy.

If the loan sharks are throwing a brick through your front window, it's time to think of something else.

Overnight success on the internet does happen but it's kind of like hitting the lottery or getting struck by lightning... it's extremely rare. So, if you need quick money, do it some other way and then come back and do something online.

Once you're able to stop thinking in terms of making instant money you'll be able to focus on something real. You'll have a chance at a legitimate online career instead of constantly searching for the next shiny-object and relying on "getting lucky."

It's time to get serious! You either want to run a legitimate online business and make steady, predictable monthly income, or you want to continue dreaming about striking it rich.

Which is it going to be?

If you choose to become a full-time online marketer, you need to *make the commitment*.

And, I'm not talking about "taking action." You hear that all the time from people who don't have a clue about online marketing but want to sound knowledgeable and impressive. They act like it's the answer to everything...

**Newbie:** "How come I can't seem to make any money online?"

**Self-proclaimed expert:** "You need to take action."

**Newbie:** "What kind of action?"

**Self-proclaimed expert:** "Massive action."

But, you know what? If you took a poll of the people spouting that advice all the time, you'd find at least 95% of them are just as broke as you are. It's like taking advice on raising children from someone who doesn't have any.

There's a big difference between taking action and making a commitment. You take action when you want to try something, when you make a *commitment* you take whatever actions are necessary and keep trying until you *get results*.

In other words, taking action will get you to the end of an idea which may-or-may-not work. But, making a commitment involves taking as many actions as necessary to get acceptable results.

So, stop thinking in terms of "taking action" and start focusing on "getting results." The results are the only thing that matters. If you commit to getting those results *no matter what*, you will automatically take action. You don't need someone to tell you about it like it's the ultimate secret to success.

## The Bottom Line

Stop thinking you're going to get rich overnight. It just doesn't work that way.

No matter what the gurus are telling you, it's never "push-button easy." There's always some work involved.

The point is… you can take massive action all day long and never get anywhere, but if you *make a commitment* you will try new things and keep going until you get the results you want.

Do *that*.

## THE BIG SECRET THE GURUS AREN'T TELLING YOU ABOUT MAKING MONEY ONLINE

Of everything you've learned—or, will learn—about online marketing there's one thing that stands out as the single most important contributing factor to your success.

The gurus know what this is and they're not telling you about it.

But, it's not because they're making a deliberate effort to hide it from you, in most cases they don't tell you because they think it's obvious and you should already know it. And, it's very likely you already do!

See... the difference is not in knowing the secret, the difference is in practicing the secret, and that's what separates the truly successful online marketers from the temporarily successful and outright failures.

And, as simple as it is, it's very difficult to genuinely practice this secret.

What's easy—and what the majority of low-level marketers fall into—is creating the illusion of the secret.

Now, I have to apologize for beating-around-the-bush a little here, but I have to go about it like this or when I reveal the secret to you you'll simply say, "pfft... who doesn't know that?," and continue to suck at online marketing for the rest of your life.

You must keep in mind that knowing the secret and not truly practicing the secret is the downfall of nearly every wannabe marketer out there. It is the reason so many people who desperately want to make money online can't do it.

OK, so now that you've been repeatedly warned about taking this concept too lightly, I'm going to reveal the secret to you.

Ready?

OK, here it is:

***Stop focusing so much on how to persuade someone to give you their money and start focusing on how you can help them solve their problems.***

That's the big secret. That's where ALL of the money is in online marketing: Helping people solve problems.

Now, I'm not saying you shouldn't put some thought into creating persuasive sales messages that entice prospects to buy your stuff, but if you can come up with new and better ways to help people solve their problems you will begin to see much more success.

Not only will you begin to make more money, but

product creation instantly becomes much easier.

Why? Because instead of thinking, *How can I get someone to give me money,* which often inspires an idea to trick or manipulate, you'll be thinking in terms of helping someone, which will inspire you to produce something valuable.

It's much easier to come up with a way to help someone than it is to come up with a way to trick someone into giving you money.

Always remember that.

If you continue to produce valuable content, people will gladly pay you for it and try to be first in line to buy your next product.

That's how a successful online marketing business is built.

Help people. That's the secret.

Now, I realize teaching such a simple and seemingly obvious concept as a "big secret" makes me look like a crackpot. But, the truth is, way too many people who would otherwise be successful are missing this crucial element.

So, please don't be one of those people who think, *I already know this... Duh...,* and continue searching for the one trick that will get people to give you money. This *is* the trick. This is what will get you money for the rest of your online marketing career.

Once people realize you're there to help them, they'll seek you out, ask you for advice and buy your products because they'll already know it won't be wasted money.

You'll get fewer refund requests and you'll spend a lot less on traffic because people will look you up. They'll hear good things about you and want to find out how they can be a part of your audience.

Not to mention, if you focus on helping people you'll start to have a better sense of self-worth. You'll begin to think of yourself as a better person because you *are* a better person. This ultimately translates into more self-confidence and greater productivity.

In this business, "making money" is a natural byproduct of helping people solve problems.

Once you truly "get" this, you'll definitely have a much better chance at success.


## But wait, there's more...

If I left off here, you'd still be way ahead of the average online marketer. However, not long after I risked looking like a crackpot by aggressively teaching this simple and seemingly obvious concept, I realized there was something else... a *Missing Element*.

So, in the next chapter, I'm going to clue you in on yet another big secret the gurus aren't telling you... only this time, instead of something that seems like it should be obvious, it's really very mind-blowing.

## THE MISSING ELEMENT

So, you put your heart and soul into creating a high-quality digital product that truly helps people solve problems, but for some reason, it really never catches on.

You see some numbskull come out of nowhere, throw together a really crappy version of your idea, doubles your price, and, BAM! He knocks it out of the park with sales.

Not only that, but Mr. Numbskull begins attracting a huge following; they can't get enough numbskullery... they follow him on facebook and twitter and when his next hastily-thrown-together product comes out, he blows it up and it becomes JVZoo's next *Product Of The Day!*

What the hell is going on?

Well, there are a number of things that could be contributing to his quick rise to fame and fortune, but there's one thing he's probably doing that you're not. I call it *The Missing Element*.

It's not because he's got a bigger list...

It's not because he's paying more for advertising...

It's not because he's a genius at writing sales copy...

It's *definitely* not because his product is better than yours...

It's because he has the audacity to assume the role of an *opinionated expert* and people see him as an authority.

But wait!, you say. I've been in this niche for 10-years and this joker stumbles in here and takes over! It doesn't make sense!

Oh, but it does. Let me explain...

## The Crazy Reason People Aren't Giving You Money

First of all, you can't just call yourself an expert and expect people to follow you into the jaws of hell; you do have to know more than the average person about your topic and have the necessary experience to back it up. But, if you've been dabbling in your niche long enough to create products and/or offer services, you probably already exceed these requirements by quite a bit.

Besides, it's not so much about your *knowledge* as it is about your *perspective*.

For example, this morning I decided to take a few minutes to learn how to use Google Calendar. So, I did what most people do in that situation: I went to YouTube and watched a few video tutorials.

There were two videos in particular that stood out to me; but, here's the interesting part: Even though both videos gave nearly identical step-by-step instructions, the presenters projected drastically different personas.

One appeared to be an actual "expert" expressing his opinion of each feature along the way; whereas the other gave the impression of a "helpful amateur" going through the very same stuff, but doing it in a much less opinionated, though admittedly clearer "click here, then there..." type of way.

If for some crazy reason I needed to hire one of these people for *Advanced Google Calendar Training*, I would definitely choose the expert over the amateur.

It would just seem wrong to pay the amateur to help me, even though both presenters proved their abilities at nearly the same level.

In fact, as far as knowledge went, in this specific case I'd probably give the edge to the amateur.

But, the expert gave me his opinion as to *why* I should or shouldn't do things a certain way. He gave me some *insight* whereas the amateur only showed me how to do stuff and where to click.

Anyone can put together a detailed, Step-by-Step training full of helpful information; but it takes an expert to give you an experienced opinion.

Look... it makes no difference that the amateur may have more actual experience than the so-called, "expert." If you're not willing to lay it on the line with your personal opinion, you're going to fall into the "helpful information" category.

People aren't looking to buy helpful information. They can find that anywhere. What they want and are more willing to pay for is your *guidance and perspective*.

Are you starting to see the major differences here?

It's important to "get" this because it's the same

*expert vs. amateur* phenomenon that's keeping you broke while less talented marketers make bank.

To raise yourself to the level of expert in the eyes of others and build authority (and make a lot more money), you need to get in the habit of offering your perspective and opinion.

You're *not* trying to trick anyone or be something you're not... *everyone* has an opinion... even you... so make sure you express it. That's really the big difference here.

And, I'm not only referring to your trainings, I'm saying you should inject this into *everything*—in your sales letters, your videos, your blog posts... put it out there on facebook and other social media. Get into it on forums.

Know your niche well enough to argue about it! Express your opinion! Force others to look to you for guidance.

Make the money you deserve...

You're the expert.

## SPEEDING UP YOUR SUCCESS

Let me start by pointing out the real value of saving time. Time is valuable—even more valuable than money—you can always get more money, but you can never get more time.

Once your time is spent, it's gone forever; so spending your time wisely is even more critical than how you spend your money.

**Money vs. Time**

Sometimes, it's smart to spend a little money if it buys you a lot of time.

For example, would you spend $10 to save 6-months of your time? I hope you answered, "Yes," because that's a no-brainer.

I'm sure you would have no problem purchasing a low-priced PDF eBook or video course if it could save you a bunch of time trying to figure out something complicated on your own.

And, if that makes sense, then why wouldn't you

spend $10 to save yourself 6-months of hard work?

I see this all the time and, when I first started out, I was guilty of it myself.

As an example, let's look at a very common scenario.

When you first start out trying to make money online, you try and do it as cheaply as possible, so you find some ClickBank products to promote.

Next, you realize you have to get traffic to the offer, but instead of wasting money on running ads, you want to see if you can get free traffic instead. After all, you don't know if the product will convert for you, so why waste money on advertising?

You conclude that if you build a blog and get it ranked on Google, you'll get free traffic all day long! Yay!

So, you spend about a week or two building the blog and filling it with content. So far, so good.

But, for some reason it's not ranking on Google so you start to do some research—you spend another week or two doing that and tweaking your blog.

You find out about link juice and spend another few weeks getting some backlinks to your site. You finally start to see some traffic come in and you're actually getting some clicks to the offer, but no one is buying.

Hmm, better build a few more pre-sell pages and maybe do a bit of article marketing.

After several months you start to get significant traffic but you're still not making sales. Or, if you're lucky, you've actually made a couple of sales, but it's not really enough money to justify the time you've put in.

After the dust settles you realize the product just doesn't convert that well for you and the next thing you know you've spent 6-months of hard work to find that out.

So, here's the gist of this lesson:

***Always be willing to spend a little money if it means saving a lot of time.***

You could have spent $10 on a facebook ad to send enough traffic to the offer to learn it doesn't convert and found that out in a matter of hours instead of wasting 6-months of your life.

Sooner or later you'll hit on something that *does* convert and then it makes sense to pursue more time-consuming free traffic methods. But, until then, save yourself 6-months of hard work and agony. If you're going to fail, you want to find out right away. Fail fast and save yourself your most valuable commodity: Time.

## Guaranteed Success

When you first start out in online marketing you need to try different things and get your feet wet. You need to see what works for you and what doesn't.

But, after you've been at it a while you need to stop experimenting and start doing something.

One of the things that will keep you in "experimentation mode" is what's known as, *the success guarantee*.

You say to yourself, "I know exactly what to do, but since it would cost money to try it, I'm not going to do it until I'm *absolutely positive* I can make a profit with it."

In other words, you want a guarantee of success before you'll commit to spending any money on a project, so nothing ever gets done.

Look... if you know "exactly what to do" but are afraid to make the investment necessary to do it correctly, then it's time to either muster up the courage to take a chance, or stop with the dream of becoming a full-time online marketer.

I know it seems like once again I'm just telling you to start spending money, but in reality I'm trying to help you.

If you don't have the money you need, that's no reason to waste 6-months of your life. Do whatever you need to do to get the necessary operating capitol.

I've been making money online for more than 20-years, but for the majority of that time, I've held a steady job along with it. I was always able to afford any tools, training or advertising I needed to make things happen.

Then one day something happened which forced me to make drastic changes in my life.

A freak accident (that I wasn't involved with) literally forced the company I worked for to close its doors overnight with no warning.

I was instantly and unexpectedly without a job.

I decided then and there I was never again going to work for someone else and I made the commitment to focus on my online marketing career.

From that moment forward I was in control of my own financial destiny.

The only problem was, at the time all this happened, I was almost dead broke.

So, you know what I did?

Well, I didn't sit down and try to figure out a bunch of free ways to do everything... I got out there and started digging through trash bins looking for bottles and cans to cash-in until I had enough to start promoting my products.

That's the truth!

And, I never did go back to work for anyone.

Seriously, this isn't about spending money, it's about getting past the unavoidable failures as quickly as possible so you can find success as quickly as possible.

If you want to start making money online and you want it to happen quickly, you're just going to have to take a few chances.

Stop trying to save small amounts of money by giving up large amounts of your time. If you're ultimately going to fail with your current project, it makes no sense to waste months of your life to find out.

Spend a few bucks to find out as soon as possible. *Fail fast*, and then move on to something else.

# YOU MUST DO THIS OR YOU WILL FAIL (NOTE: YOU'RE NOT DOING THIS!)

## The Lifeblood Of Your Business

If you've been around online marketing forums you already know "The money's in the list." But, I'm going to go even further and tell you that everything you do online, whether it's blogging or selling eBooks, should be done with the intention of putting people on an email list. And, that intention should be the number one goal of everything you do online.

Your list is everything. It's your whole business. Without an email list you are destined to fade out faster than Dick Cheney's signature on a charity donation.

Stop thinking only in terms of how much you can make from your product; you've also got to consider the steady income you'll receive from the resulting list. That's how you'll build a sustainable online business. There's no other way.

If you're truly serious about becoming a full-time online marketer, you *must* build a list or you will fail.

Everyone that reads this should get familiar with autoresponders and study email marketing.

Now, don't get caught up with "which autoresponder is the best?" type of questions. When I first started learning about building email lists, I spent an entire week trying to decide whether I should go with GetResponse or Aweber.

Many years later, after having used both of them I can report they're both really good and you should spend no more than 30-minutes checking out their web sites and making a decision.

What I *will* recommend is that you do NOT go with a free autoresponder service.

Why?

Because free autoresponders are going to ultimately force you to switch to a paid plan anyway as soon as your list becomes big enough to build a business, and free autoresponders tend to have inferior delivery rates.

What difference does it make if it's free or not if your emails don't reach your email subscriber? It's worthless!

Now, I've heard that the limited free version of Mail Chimp in particular has a pretty good delivery rate, but others I've seen do not. Once you get a decent sized list the last thing you'll want to do is have to change autoresponders because of crappy delivery rates.

Also, what if your free autoresponder decides it can't sustain itself and goes out of business? Then you've lost all your contacts and are out of business as well.

There's one other reason to use one of the two autoresponders I recommend: nearly every third-party software supports them.

For example, if you need to integrate your

autoresponder into your membership plugin, it's usually already set up for those two autoresponders. Just click on the Aweber or GetResponse option and it's already set-up for you.

But, what happens if you're using *Uncle Harry's Fly-By-Night Autoresponder Service* (or, in some cases, even Mail Chimp)? Well, unfortunately, you'll play hell trying to get plugins to work with it because it's not supported.

If you're nervous about signing up for a paid autoresponder service and having to commit to a monthly fee, let me put your mind at ease. GetResponse offers a free 30-day trial and recently, Aweber has ditched their $1 trial and replaced it with a free trial as well. So, get in there and play around with each of them and decide which one trips your trigger.

Personally, I think Aweber is easier to use and an all-around better autoresponder, but GetResponse is quickly gaining ground and seems to be more accepting of email marketers (and, for that reason, I'm using GetResponse these days).

I get the feeling Aweber would prefer you only run a cute little mom-and-pop newsletter operation from their service and they maniacally recommend and practically force you to use "double op-in" subscriptions. *D'oh!*

At any rate, your business rides on the email list and having a sub-par service is way too risky. Go with either GetResponse or Aweber (or Infusionsoft if you're rich).

Now, if you're currently on my list, you might notice my emails are coming from something called, SendGrid or Send13.

That's because I've been trying out the built-in autoresponder that comes with the full Etison suite at

ClickFunnels. SendGrid and Send13 are their recommended SMTP servers.

I like the idea of having all my sales funnels, page builders, autoresponders, and affiliate mechanism in one place. ClickFunnels makes a lot of sense for me (or anyone, really), but it might be a bit hard to justify the price until you reach a certain income level.

If you *do* want to check out ClickFunnels, you can get a free 14-day trial by going through my personal affiliate link:

**http://DigitalProgressReport.com/click14**

Anyway, I haven't given up on GetResponse; I still maintain several lists there as well.

## The Standard Procedure

Once you decide on your autoresponder service it's time to focus on what type of content you should send to your list. The ultimate answer of course, is to set up a one or two-week autoresponder series to give them whatever you think would help them the most. Get them used to receiving useful content so you not only help them, but train them to open your emails.

You want them to actually *look forward* to receiving your emails!

This should be your goal whether you got them on your list through a free lead magnet or through a sale.

However, if you're getting subscribers through a purchase of some sort, I think it's a good idea to come up with an email sequence similar to the following:

EMAIL ONE: Thank them for purchasing your product and briefly introduce yourself.

EMAIL TWO: Give them an unadvertised bonus of some sort. It can be a related free PDF download or simply a link to a video you've prepared for them—just make sure it's something related and helpful to what you've sold them.

EMAIL THREE: Give them some more useful content related to the thing you've sold them.

EMAIL FOUR: Again, send them some more useful content related to what you've sold them, but also related to something you want to promote. Consider something that would be the next logical step after they've consumed your product. For example, if you've sold them a PDF eBook about how to get ranked on Google, give them a tip on keyword research and then mention a software tool that automates the process (either something of yours or something in which you receive an affiliate commission).

I'm sure you get the idea. You'll have to tailor your email sequences to your particular business and niche.

After your autoresponder sequence has run its course, it's time to switch gears.

I personally don't believe the initial autoresponder sequence should last longer than one… maybe two-weeks, tops… and then you should start sending out daily broadcast emails you write from scratch every day.

I also believe your daily broadcast emails should always promote something; either some other product of yours or an affiliate product.

Now, I don't mean send out spammy, "Hey! Buy this

thing!" type of promotions; you should still send out useful, informative and hopefully entertaining content, but that content should also transition into a way for you to earn some money.

Start your emails by telling a story or solving a problem, then tie-in to the promotion at the end.

For example, if you're going to promote a WordPress Security plugin, you could start your email by telling the story of how you or someone you know got hacked and then give them the solution along with your affiliate link.

## Why Experienced Marketers Tend To Pee Their Pants Over This Advice

You hear so many pros tell you to build a list that the advice almost blows past you. You're probably sick of hearing it and at this point it just sounds like a TV tuned to a dead channel.

But, there's a reason you hear such big name online marketers—those who you'd think would have better things to do—give you that same advice over and over…

It's because after trying everything else, they've learned it's literally the only online money-making idea that consistently makes money every single day; therefore, it's the only legitimate business model choice you have.

Let me give you the classic example. Let's say you've built your list to 1,000 subscribers. So, how much is each subscriber worth to you each month?

As a general rule, your list should produce about $1 per subscriber.

The number will be different depending on the niche and skill of the person writing the emails—but $1 is easy to work with and we don't need to get too precise for this explanation.

It also changes depending on the various offers you'll be promoting. But, we're going to go with the classic example here in order to make things simple.

The reason you see that one-dollar figure used so much is because it's kind of the low-bar average. If you're not making at least $1 per subscriber each month after attaining 1,000 subscribers, you'd better take a strong look at your email marketing skills or move into another niche.

Anyway, here's how the math breaks down when you send your monthly emails to 1,000 subscribers (using average statistics published by various autoresponder companies):

**Open rates average about 20%, so:**

*1,000 subs x .20 = 200 opens per email sent*

**Clickthrough rates (CTR) average about 30%, so:**

*200 opens x .30 = 60 clicks*

**Earnings-per-click (EPC) will vary depending on the offer, but let's use the low-bar figure of one-dollar, so:**

*$1 x 60 = $60 per email*

**If you send an average of 4-promotional-emails per week it comes out to:**

*4 x $60 = $240 per week*

**With an average of 4.33 weeks in a month (this is pretty close if you do the math), you will make:**

*4.33 x $240 = $1,039.20 per month.*

**If you're making $1,039.20 per month and you have 1,000 subscribers:**

*$1,039.20 ÷ 1,000 = approximately $1.04 per subscriber*

That's basically the breakdown explaining the $1 per-subscriber figure you see thrown around all the time.

Now, if you've got a honkin' 150,000-subscriber list, the average numbers above will most-likely go down because it's a lot harder to prune and nurture a list of that size, but if you're reading this report, that's probably not you.

Anyway, if you're averaging $1 per subscriber each month, how many subscribers should you try to get?

The answer, of course, is...

AS MANY AS POSSIBLE!

Can you imagine what life would be like if you *did* have 150,000 subscribers?

And, the funniest thing of all is you don't even need to have your own product!

You can build a list like this and make a lot of money simply by putting up a squeeze page offering a FREE VIDEO revealing something cool in exchange for an email address. Then, use the resulting list to promote affiliate products!

Isn't that neat?

And, it's even easier than you think... you don't even need to create the lead-magnet video yourself! Just find an informative video on YouTube that teaches something important in your niche and then embed that video on your *thank you* page.

When someone signs-up, have your "welcome" email explain the reason that particular video "changed your life," or whatever fits, then follow-up with your autoresponder series.

So, what are *you* going to be doing this afternoon?

I thought so. ☺


## Your Primary Mission

Having gone all through this stuff boils down to one simple concept:

***Everything you do in your online business should be geared toward getting people on a***

**list.**

There is no other option if you want to be a full-time online marketer. You've heard it a million times but it's the truth: *The money's in the list.*

Many gurus have said having a good, responsive email list is like having your personal ATM machine or a license to print money. I'm not sure I'd go that far, but it's definitely fun to click the send button and watch your bank account increase.

Learn to get good at email marketing because that's what you're really going to be doing for the life of your online marketing career. It's important to create high-quality products, but the email list will be the lifeblood of your business.

## AFFILIATE MARKETING ISN'T A VIABLE BUSINESS MODEL UNLESS...

Affiliate marketing is simply promoting someone else's product to get a piece of the profit. The first question you have to ask is why someone would be willing to split the profit with you—and, often give you a larger percentage than they give themselves—just for promoting their product?

Well, part of the reason is something called *Customer Lifetime Value* (which we will learn about later). If they know their numbers, they know they'll be adding a customer to their list and can sometimes even give up over 100% of the profit on the front end to make many multiples of that over the lifetime of their customer relationship.

It's a great deal for them because they only have to pay for *customers*, not advertising. Normally, when you buy advertising, you have to pay for every click or every ad impression whether or not someone becomes a customer.

It's also a great deal for you because you get to share in the profit without having to create a product yourself.

Sounds like a total win-win, right? After all, you don't have to do anything but send people to the sales page using your affiliate link and sit back and collect money. What could be easier than that?

In fact, it *is* a great deal for you. Unfortunately, almost no one does it correctly.

The correct way to do affiliate marketing—and actually make money doing it—is actually a lot of hard work.

What most people do is build a website, stick a bunch of affiliate links all over the place and then hope someone clicks on them and buys the promoted product. But, guess what? It is a rarely happens that way.

Usually, what happens is you'll get clicks to the promotion, but no one ever buys.

Is it because the product owner is screwing you out of your commissions?

Well, it's easy to think that way because, after all, you're sending plenty of traffic and surely someone should have bought the product, right?

But, that's not the reason. The product owner isn't screwing you out of your commissions; you're screwing yourself out of commissions by using a faulty affiliate marketing plan.

Building a website and sticking a bunch of affiliate links all over it is almost never going to work, and if it does work, you're screwing yourself out of gobs of cash—maybe even 100-times what you'd be making if you did it right.

But, don't worry; I'm going to explain the right way to do it. If you follow my advice for affiliate marketing, you'll make plenty of cash.

## Why You're Not Making Money

If you're already doing affiliate marketing you probably started with it because it seems like easy money… just send people to the offer through your affiliate link and when someone buys you get a commission.

The problem, though, is that people rarely buy the first time they see a product. They have to think about it for a while or even search for some reviews to make sure they're not making a mistake. What if it's junk? What if there is a better product that does the same thing? What if there's a better deal somewhere else? What if there's something out there for free that's just as good? Etc.

There's trust and social proof issues going on as well. The bottom line is that people generally don't buy something on the first visit to the offer page. What tends to happen is you send them to the offer, they decide they might want to buy, then they go to Google and start researching.

The next thing you know they find a review site somewhere that satisfies their concerns and they click through on *that* site's affiliate link and you lose your commission.

Another thing that happens is the prospect knows it's an affiliate link and either reloads the page without your link or replaces it with their own affiliate link so they get the commission instead of you (which, by the way, isn't allowed through most affiliate programs).

This especially happens a lot with "make money online" products because people who buy that kind of stuff know all about affiliate links.

So, what's the solution?

Unfortunately, there's no way to stop someone if they're determined to replace your link with theirs, but you can drastically help your chances of success by plugging one of the most common leaks...

## Using Redirects

The first thing you should do is use a redirect for your links (this is sometimes called "cloaking" or "masking" links.)

Below you'll see a standard hoplink from ClickBank and what the same link would look like when masked by a redirect.

I randomly chose a product from ClickBank called, *Penny Stock Prophet*.

IMPORTANT NOTE: I'm not in any way endorsing or recommending that product.

Seriously. I've never even looked at it!

I know absolutely nothing about the stock market and you'd be sorely disappointed if you took that type of advice from me.

It's just the first thing I saw at ClickBank while writing this section.

OK, I think I've made that clear. Let's get back to redirects...

Compare the two links below. The first one is what ClickBank spit-up for an affiliate link. The second one is a made-up domain name and doesn't actually work but I wanted to give you an idea of what a redirected link would look like:

**Affiliate Link:**

http://6d883q-0n43e-j8bi7p8n4kueh.hop.clickbank.net/

**Redirect Link:**

http://yoursite.com/pennystocks

These are both the same link. As you can see, the redirect link is not only nicer and more compact, it also doesn't alert the visitor they're about to click on an affiliate link.

Also, on a psychological level, the first link looks scary, like it could be sending you to a malicious web site or something. If nothing else, you'll get more traffic sent to the offer with a redirect because it uses your own domain name and it looks like they're simply going to a different page on your website.

Even if you use anchor text such as **CLICK HERE** people often hover over the link to reveal the destination URL and it still makes a difference in clickthrough rates.

When I first replaced all my links with redirects, I noticed a major increase in clickthroughs. I was amazed and it was only then that I started to make some decent affiliate income. Take my word for it, it makes a big difference.

A second reason to use redirects is so you can track how much traffic you're getting to each link. If you have several links on a web page all going to the same offer, you'll be able to see which link is the most successful.

This is useful information because you'll be able to tweak or remove the bad links and replace them with something more effective.

Still, a third reason to use redirects is because you can change the landing page destination very quickly. You might have 50-links spread-out all over the internet promoting an Amazon product and then, suddenly, Amazon discontinues that product or a newer version comes out. You don't want to have to try and find all those links, and then change them manually; it would be much simpler to just change the redirect destination once and BANG!—All 50-links are instantly updated.

So, how do you create a redirect? Well, there are several ways you can do it. I've done it just about every possible way. I could show you how to manually code a redirect link and upload it to your server, or change the htaccess file on your WordPress blog, but there are much simpler solutions.

If you're a small-time WordPress user it's easy: simply do a Google search for **free wordpress redirect plugin.**

However, if you're not using WordPress, or even if you are and you're serious enough about affiliate marketing to want some critical features not found in any of the free plugins, I have two major recommendations for you:

The first is by far the best and you can get a free version, but it's going to cost you a monthly fee if you want to use a custom domain name.

It's called, *ClickMeter*. With ClickMeter, you can do everything from tracking conversions & revenue to split-testing. It's super powerful and if you're super serious or using something like ClickFunnels, it's really the only way to go.

ClickMeter also works with any other type of website—including WordPress—but, it takes some extra tech-work on your part if you want to use your own domain name as part of the link.

For me, that's not really a problem, but if you're not comfortable working with nameservers and DNS records and the general sound of that idea causes you to break-out into a cold sweat, maybe you should pass on that one.

Honestly, it's not as difficult as it sounds and there are always detailed step-by-step instructions you can follow.

My second recommendation is *Easy Redirect Script*. It's got some features that I think are indispensable when trying to make money with affiliate marketing and you can use it whether or not you're using WordPress.

Easy Redirect Script doesn't have nearly the features and none of the analytics of ClickMeter, but it's miles ahead of all the free options.

Not only does it let you control what your affiliate link looks like, it also allows you to control what the destination URL looks like on the landing page!

For example, if you followed my affiliate link for Penny Stock Prophet you'd see this as the destination URL in your browser:

pennystockprophet.com/?hop=truebonus

"truebonus" is my affiliate I.D. How easy would it be for someone to backspace over it and reload the page as this?:

pennystockprophet.com

If that website didn't properly cookie my affiliate code on the visitor's device or if they're using some kind of "cookie blocker," I'm instantly going to lose my commission.

But, what if instead of seeing...

pennystockprophet.com/?hop=truebonus

at the top of their browser, they were presented with:

mysite.com/pennystocks

What I just showed you there is called a "stealth redirect." It changes the *destination* URL to match your redirect link, and this feature, among several others, is included in Easy Redirect Script.

With a stealth redirect there's no way they can easily reload the sales page without my affiliate code, at least not without some inconvenient research on where the page actually resides. It probably isn't going to stop someone determined to replace your affiliate ID with theirs, but it will stop someone whose only motive is to kill your commissions.

There are all kinds of other goodies included with Easy Redirect Script, but if I shared them all here you'd accuse me of a full-blown promotion and, besides, we've got a lot of other ground to cover in this chapter.

If you want further information about Easy Redirect Script and all the cool things it can do you can watch this 1-hour webinar replay presented by the developers:

http://digitalprogressreport.com/erswebinar

Replacing all your affiliate links with redirects is a must if you're serious about making money as an affiliate marketer. But, there's a whole lot more you can do to increase your chances of success, so let's move on...

**Creating A Lead Magnet For Affiliate Marketing**

In the previous chapter I explained that everything you do online should be geared toward getting prospects on a list. Well, this is no exception; in fact, this is probably the *best case ever* for creating a list.

But, by definition, affiliate marketing is selling *other people's* products. How are you going to get prospects on a list if you don't have your own product?

The answer is you need to set up a squeeze page offering a good lead magnet.

The good news is that it only has to be a *One Problem, One Solution* type of lead magnet. In fact, it has to be.

Let me explain...

Not all lead magnets are created equal. The specific kind of lead magnet you offer is *critical* to being a successful affiliate marketer, so pay extra close attention here.

When you create your lead magnet it *actually works against you* if you give them a complete product. What you want to do is give them a small piece of the overall solution in order to compel them to buy the rest from you in the form of the product you're promoting.

That's not to say what you're going to give them doesn't work for them, it must be a valuable piece of the overall puzzle, it's just not the complete puzzle.

In other words, we want to scratch an itch, but not completely stop all the itching, if you know what I mean. So, let me give you an example:

Let's say I want to promote a product called, *Sales Funnel Extravaganza* (I know, it's a lame-ass name, but that's not important right now). The product itself might have the following modules:

1. How to design your sales funnel
2. How to create a lead magnet
3. How to set up your autoresponder
4. How to set up a squeeze page
5. How to create a saleable product
6. How to write a sales letter
7. How to set up your sales page
8. How to create an upsell
9. How to set up your upsell page
10. How to set up an autoresponder series
11. How to write email offers
12. Putting it all together

OK, I just threw that together, but I'm sure you catch my drift. If we were promoting a product teaching all those things, our lead magnet might consist of something like a 5-page PDF with the totally original title of, *How to Make Money Online*.

So, now, in our lead magnet we basically explain the way to make money online is to create a sales funnel. We tell them what it is, and get them excited about it, but we don't tell them how to do it. For that, they'll need to purchase our promoted product and we start sending them emails promoting that product.

We actually give them a valuable and good explanation on how a sales funnel works—something that satisfies their itch about how to make money online—but, at the same time we're leading them into temptation.

Now that they know the secret to making money online is with a sales funnel, they need instruction on the individual elements of creating that sales funnel and all that goes with it. In other words, they need the product we're promoting.

We didn't rip them off; we gave them good, valuable information. We explained the complete *method* for making money online, but we didn't give them the "how-to." For that, they need the product.

While we're on the subject, though, don't even think about pulling this kind of crap with a product they've already paid for.

When someone pays for one of your products, you have got to give them a complete system. You don't ever want to sell a product that won't stand on its own without having to buy something else.

You could sell your PDF that teaches them how to manually extract keywords and then upsell software that does it automatically. There's nothing wrong with that, but you can't sell something that basically says, "The first step is to also buy my software."

OK, back to affiliate marketing…

## Offering Bonuses

Another thing you can do to increase your affiliate marketing success is to offer a bonus for purchasing through your affiliate link.

If you followed my advice and got your prospects on a list, you can email them and explain that if they purchase a certain product though your link, you'll give them a related product for free.

Taking the example from the end of the last section, we could promote the keyword software while offering a related PDF as a bonus for purchasing through our link.

If you're promoting a product on JVZoo and your bonus is something like a PDF (or, any downloadable product under 128mb) you can upload your bonus so they'll automatically get it when they purchase through your link.

Just go to the AFFILIATES tab and click on AFFILIATE BONUSES and upload your bonus for the desired promotion (you have to be an approved affiliate for that product first, though).

If you're promoting products on other platforms, you'll have to tell the customer to email a copy of their receipt so you can verify they purchased through your link. If everything checks out, you send them the link to download the bonus.

What works really well is to give them a workable method for using the purchased product. For example, if you're promoting the keyword software mentioned above, you could offer a case study of how you used that software to make x-amount of dollars and explain how, after they learn your method, they could do it too.

The only drawback to offering bonuses like this is the confusion that comes with it. You're going to get people that don't realize they need to purchase specifically through your link to get the bonus and get upset when they find out they're not getting it. The best advice I can give you is to make it crystal clear they *must buy through your link to get the bonus!*

## Broken Record (let me drill it into your head one last time)

In this chapter I went through the importance of masking your links, offering bonuses, creating an effective lead magnet and getting prospects on an email list.

The email list is by far the most important. I know I sound like a broken record, but you must get people on a list to make money online regardless of whether you're offering your own product or promoting affiliate products.

If you find some other way of making good money online without building a list—that's great—but, you should *still* find a way to build that list and *make even more* money.

Starting with the next chapter, we're going to "kick-it-up-a-notch" and go all *mathematical* on you. ☺

## TIME TO BREAK OUT THE CALCULATOR

This book deals with the truth. And, when you're dealing with the truth you need science to back it up. Unfortunately, that means we're going to have to use math.

Math isn't fun. It scares a lot of people away, so you rarely see this stuff taught in an online marketing product. But, I'm here to tell you it's essential if you plan on making a living as an online marketer.

If I had my "druthers," I'd put the "math stuff" in the very back of this book because it's unlikely to inspire the kind of enthusiasm I normally shoot for in the opening sections of my trainings.

Believe me, if there were a way to hide this stuff more toward the back, I would have. But, the inconvenient reality is that so much of what follows depends on the reader understanding the 10-essential business calculations.

If you want to run a full-time online business it's critical you learn this stuff. There is no other way.

I honestly don't believe it's possible to run a sustained

online marketing business without knowing this stuff. So, as eye-glazing as it might be to some readers, let's just do it and get it over with.

## How To Calculate Percentages

Even if you already know how to calculate percentages, it might be a good idea to read this section so you can more easily follow along with the specific methods we'll be using. I promise it will be quick (only about 1-page of content).

To start off with, let's look at the word *percent*. What it means, literally, is "per-hundred." *Cent* is based on the Latin word for "hundred."

The prefix *per* means "for each" or "divided by."

For example, 15-percent means 15-one-hundredths, or 15-divided-by-100. Another shorthand way to represent "divided by" is to use the slash "/". So, in this case, it would be 15/100 (literally, 15 divided by 100).

Let's do that... let's divide 15 by 100. We get 0.15, right? Easy, peasy. But, what does that mean? If we were talking about one U.S. dollar, we would be talking about 15-cents. Remember, "cent" means "hundred" and there are 100-cents to every dollar. So, 15% of a dollar is 15-cents (0.15)

What's confusing to a lot of people is when percentages are applied to numbers other than 100, like: "What is 15-percent of 45?"

Imagine you had $45. We want to know how much money would represent 15% of those dollars, so let's start with getting a number we can work with:

15% means 15-divided-by-100 so, 15 ÷ 100 equals 0.15

We can work with 0.15, right?

To calculate 15% of $45 we simply multiply 0.15 x 45 and get $6.75.

15% of $45 is $6.75.

How about 8% of $175? Well, 8 ÷ 100 equals 0.08, so 0.08 x 175 = $14

Want more? (don't answer that):

13% of $25? 0.13 x 25 = $3.25

42% of $950 = $399

42% of $9.50 = $3.99 (see what we did there?) ☺

Anyhow, I think you get the idea. If not, go back through this section one more time and I'm sure you will. By-the-way, this is probably the most complicated calculation you'll encounter in this whole book, so if you got through this part, you're fully-primed to learn the rest.

# SECTION TWO

# ESSENTIAL MARKETING MATHEMATICS

Including The Ten Calculations Every Online Marketer Needs To Know

## TEN CALCULATIONS EVERY MARKETER NEEDS TO KNOW

Now that you're up to speed on all the preliminary math involved, it's time to go through the specific calculations you'll be using on a regular basis in your online marketing business.

Some of these calculations are used more than others, but it would be rare for an online marketer to not use all of them at some point.

Unfortunately, this is liable to be a long, boring, and possibly frustrating section for you, but it's not something you can really skip, OK?

Successful online marketing is all about the math. If you truly hate math you really only have two options:

Either you can learn to do it yourself.

Or...

Hire someone to do it for you.

There really isn't any other way. Everything you do online will have a mathematical component to it.

Even if you're planning on hiring someone to handle

the math for you, I still recommend you go through this section and at least understand how it all works.

Otherwise how will you know if you hired someone capable or not?

Anyway, I'll put each calculation on its own page to keep things neat and orderly.

The first of the calculations, *Contribution to Overhead*, begins on the next page...

## 1. CONTRIBUTION TO OVERHEAD

**Abbreviation:** *CTO*

**Calculation:** *Product price minus fixed costs*

In order to correctly explain Contribution to Overhead (CTO) I have to go offline and give you an example from the mail-order business, also known as the Direct Response business. Anyway, here's a quote from one of my favorite Direct Marketing books, Vincent James' *The 12-Month Millionaire*:

*"CTO is what your business will net after you pay for goods sold. Out of this CTO, you still have to pay for advertising, postage, employees, etc."*

In other words, CTO is the profit you can expect for each unit sold after you deduct what it cost to directly produce the product.

But, that's for physical products being sold through mail order. In the digital world, I use it this way: I take the selling price of the product and deduct any fixed fees that will always apply to every product sold. For example, I will find out what it will cost to sell my product through a payment processor like *PayPal* and a digital marketplace such as JVZoo.

PayPal and JVZoo are going to take their cut no matter what. I might offer my product for sale on

Warrior Forum's WSO section, or I might run a facebook ad; either way, PayPal and JVZoo will still get a percentage of each sale, AND it will be a fixed dollar-amount as long as I sell my product at a fixed price (we're not going to complicate this discussion by considering ever-increasing "dime-sales", etc.)

So, let's say we are selling a 20-page PDF eBook for $7. Before we even decide where or how we're going to sell it, we should calculate our *Contribution to Overhead* so we know exactly how much money we can expect for each sale.

There's lots of ways we could set up our sales process, but when I sell a PDF eBook, I very often go through JVZoo and PayPal, so let me show you how to do the calculation that way.

Our eBook sells for $7 and JVZoo is going to take 5% of every sale, so:

$7 x .05 = 35-cents.

PayPal takes 2.9% plus 30-cents for every sale, so:

$7 x .029 = 21-cents (after rounding up) + 30-cents = 51-cents

So, the combined fees will total 86-cents (35-cents for JVZoo and 51-cents for PayPal).

In this example, our $7 eBook will net us $6.14 ($7 minus 86-cents) and that's our CTO.

We don't figure-in things like advertising cost or the cost to post a WSO on Warrior Forum because those things will vary from campaign to campaign—the profit from the eBook will always stay the same.

Knowing your Contribution to Overhead is important because you'll need it to accurately calculate everything else associated with selling your product. We'll see how it works as we go through some of the other calculations in this book.

## 2. BREAK EVEN POINT

**Abbreviation:** *BEP*

**Calculation:** *Number of units you must sell to break-even for the current campaign*

Once we get our Contribution to Overhead (CTO) number, we can start working with it to lay out strategies to make money. However, our first stop isn't so sexy. We need to see what it's going to take to *break even*.

This is important because we don't have money to just throw around on a campaign and hope it works. We have to evaluate our chances of at least breaking even before we try something.

For example, at the time I'm writing this, it costs $20 to run a WSO on Warrior Forum. So, at a CTO of $6.14, how many eBooks do we have to sell to break even?

The answer is 3.26 ($20 ÷ $6.14 = 3.26). And, since we can't sell a fractional portion of our eBook (.26 to be exact), we'll have to sell the whole thing which brings us up to 4.

So, for this example, our Break Even Point (BEP) is 4.

The reason why this is important to calculate is so you can contemplate the success of a campaign. A WSO costs $20 and the question you have to ask yourself is, *can I realistically sell 4 copies of my eBook to try it out?*

From my own experience in selling WSOs and

reading the comments of others, I think a break-even point of 4 is worth a shot for a first-time WSO. I think I sold 6 copies of my first WSO the first time I posted it, then several more after the reviews came in and I bumped it a few times (reposting is called, "bumping" on the WF).

First-timers often have a tough time selling on the Warrior Forum because no one knows who you are and it's hard to sell a "make money online" product if you've never made any money online.

So, in general I wouldn't recommend trying a WSO if you have no experience (but, it is possible, and we will discuss that possibility later on in section four, *Radioactive Seeds*).

Anyhow, for the record, I'd like to say I think it's worth trying to sell a WSO even if you sell NO copies at all. Why? Because the experience you'll gain is worth ten-times what you'd pay to post it.

Now, to be clear, you wouldn't want to try and sell a "make money online" product if you have no experience making money online, but if you did follow one of the legitimate ways to do it in Radioactive Seeds, it's definitely worth the learning experience even if you didn't make any sales.

OK, getting back to the *Break-Even Point*. We decided that 4 was a doable number and worth the risk. But, what if the Warrior Forum decided to increase the price of posting a WSO to $40? This isn't out of the question because, since the new owners took over, there's been a lot of price testing and the cost of posting a WSO really was $40 just a few months before I originally wrote this section.

So, if the cost was $40, how many eBooks would we have to sell to break even? The answer is 6.51 or 7 after rounding up. Now, the decision is a little tougher because newbies rarely sell more than about 3 or 4 copies of their first WSO, if any. You have a really good chance of NOT reaching your goal of 7-sales the first time around (that's not to say you won't sell a whole lot more after the reviews come in and you bump it a few times).

But, that's why we calculate a Break Even Point in the first place: to make an informed estimate of the risk involved. Personally, for my first product, I'd do it just for the experience and chalk-up any losses to lessons learned. But, that's how I roll; you might not think blowing $40 is worth it to waste on such lessons.

The bottom line is that you should always calculate your BEP when evaluating a new campaign. Don't look at it after the fact and say, "Holy guacamole! I needed to sell 300-copies to break even! No wonder I lost my ass!"

## 3. CONVERSION RATE

**Abbreviation:** *CR*

**Calculation:** *Percentage of visitors (or actions) that reach the desired action*

*Conversion Rate* (CR) is one of those calculations that can be applied to many different outcomes.

For example, it can be applied to an opt-in scenario in which the desired action is to *convert* the visitor into a lead, or it can be applied to a sales scenario in which the desired action is to *convert* the visitor into a customer.

When calculating a conversion rate, the first thing you have to do is define the *desired action*. In other words, what is it you want to have happen?

The first time I tried to barbeque hamburgers, I had a pretty crappy conversion rate—I ended up burning about eight-out-of-ten of them. So, considering my desired action was to produce an edible hamburger patty, my conversion rate was only about 20% (only 2 out of 10 reached the desired action).

Now, 20% is a horrible conversion rate for cooking hamburgers, but it's a pretty good conversion rate when you're talking about sales.

If I sent 100 visitors to a sales page and 20 of them made a purchase, it would be a 20% conversion rate. That would be excellent considering the typical sales conversion rate is only around 1 or 2 percent.

So, how are we calculating these conversion rates?

We're simply dividing the *desired actions* by the *overall actions*.

In the example above, we are taking the number of desired actions, which was 20, and dividing it by the overall actions which was 100.

So, the calculation looks like this: 20 divided by 100 or 20/100 = .20 or 20%

If only 2 visitors made a purchase out of 100 it would look like this: 2/100 = .02 or 2%.

Let's try it again, only this time let's say we sent 100 visitors to an opt-in page and 40 of them reached the desired action and opted-in.

In this example the conversion rate is 40% (40/100 = .40 or 40%).

If you sent a total of 1,286 visitors to a sales page and 27 of them made a purchase then your conversion rate would be:

27/1286 = .02099... or a little over 2%

I don't think you need this drilled into your head any further than this; it's really pretty simple. In fact, you've already done this calculation way at the beginning where I showed you how to calculate percentages.

A conversion rate is just a percentage: the percentage of desired actions.

So, just to be clear, the way to calculate Conversion Rate is to take the number of *desired* actions and divide it by the number of *overall* actions.

And, away we go...

## 4. RETURN ON INVESTMENT

**Abbreviation:** *ROI*
**Calculation:** *Average percent return per campaign unit expense*

OK, so now that we've figured out our CTO, BEP and CR, the next stop on our quest is *Return on Investment* (ROI). This is where most newbies try to start. However, we are smarter than most and already have a few other critical calculations under our belt.

We can calculate a ROI using the WSO model from the previous chapter, but it will make more sense and be easier to explain if we go with a pay-per-click model. This is where we buy ads on a website and the cost of doing so is based on the number of clicks we get.

Let's keep our CTO at $6.14 just to keep things consistent. I would almost never try to run a pay-per-click campaign for a product that sells for so little, mainly because it's going to be hard to make any money with it. However, it isn't impossible and later on we'll see how it would definitely make sense in certain circumstances (and, no, I'm not just talking about list building).

Facebook offers several ways you can run ads including a pay-per-click model, but you'll be hard pressed to run one that costs you less than 25-cents a click when you promote an off-site property. That's just not realistic when you're trying to sell a $7 product with a CTO of $6.14.

In the past, I have gotten the price down to 6-cents a click and that would be more reasonable, but, as we shall see, it's probably not good enough to make a comfortable profit.

But, this section isn't about how to get cheap clicks, it's about how to calculate your ROI, so let's get back on track.

Let's run a few numbers and see how ROI works. In the first scenario, let's say we're getting 10-cent clicks to our sales letter. Let's also say we will get a somewhat typical 2% conversion. That means for every 100 visitors to our sales letter, we'll sell, on average, 2 eBooks.

Since we make $6.14 on each sale, we will make $12.28 for every 100 visitors on average. So, at 10-cents a click, a hundred visitors will cost us $10.

Now we have all the info we need to calculate ROI. For every 100 visitors we will make, on average, $2.28 ($12.28 for selling 2 eBooks minus $10.00 in ad spend).

The easy way to calculate ROI is to take the profit for 100 clicks ($2.28) and divide it by what it cost us to get those 100 clicks ($10).

$2.28 divided by $10 equals .228. So, our ROI is 22.8%.

Now that we know our ROI we can predict how much we will make for a given ad spend. Let's say we wanted to send 1,000 clicks to our landing page. That would cost us $100; so, at a 22.8% ROI we can expect to make a $22.80 profit!

$100 x .228 = $22.80

But, let's try another scenario. Let's say it cost us 25-cents a click instead. In that case, it would cost us $25 to get those 100 visitors.

Now the calculation would go like this:

We sold 2 eBooks at a $6.14 CTO for a total of $12.28, but it cost us $25 to run the ads. $25 minus $12.28 equals a $12.72 *loss*!

We still run the calculation the same way, but it will be a negative ROI when we're done: $12.72 divided by $25 equals .5088 or about a -50.9% negative ROI.

With an ROI this bad it wouldn't make sense to send more clicks, so we would stop our ad and reevaluate what went wrong. It might be that we could redo our landing page to get a higher conversion, say 5%. That might do it. Let's see:

5% conversion means we would sell 5 eBooks per 100-visitors at a CTO of $6.14 equals $30.70. Now we are back in the positive and our ROI would be:

$30.70 - $25 = $5.70 divided by $25 equals .228 or a positive ROI of 22.8%

Yay!

It might be that you'll never get that good of a conversion rate. In that case, you'll have to look elsewhere to turn around a negative campaign. You can try to get the cost-per-click down or you might try a product price increase. There are a number of things you could do; you'll just have to start testing.

OK, on to the next calculation...

## 5. PROSPECT ACQUISITION COST

**Abbreviation:** *PAC*

**Calculation:** *Cost of getting a visitor to your landing page*

This is a *really* simple calculation, but it's something you should know about and keep track of, so I'll show it to you here real quick.

It's simply the cost involved with getting someone to visit your landing page. So, if you're running a pay-per-click ad campaign and it cost you 10-cents a click, then your *Prospect Acquisition Cost* (PAC) is going to be 10-cents. Simple.

But, let's say you're running another type of ad, one that you pay for impressions rather than clicks.

In general, you pay in terms of 1,000 impressions—in other words, your ad is shown 1,000 times (and, unfortunately, it's not necessarily shown to 1,000 different people).

Anyhow, let's say you spend $10 for 1,000 impressions. That's only 1-cent per impression! Not bad, right?

Well, don't get too excited yet... in order to know if it's a good deal or not we need to keep track of how many clicks we get.

If we were to get 100 clicks out of those 1,000 impressions, it would mean we are paying 10-cents a click just as when we used the pay-per-click model above.

But, if we were to get 200 clicks out of those 1,000 impressions, it would be much better... we'd be getting 5-cent clicks and our Prospect Acquisition Cost would be 5-cents.

OK, I think you've got the idea. Let's move on...

## 6. CUSTOMER ACQUISITION COST

**Abbreviation:** *CAC*

**Calculation:** *The cost to acquire a customer*

This is similar to *Prospect Acquisition Cost* except it's the cost involved in acquiring a *customer* (someone who actually bought your product).

So, let's say it cost us $10 to get 100 customers to our sales page and 2 actually purchased our eBook. In this scenario, we would take the total cost, which is $10 and divide it by 2 since that's how many customers we acquired:

$10 divided by 2 = $5

We have a *Customer Acquisition Cost* (CAC) of $5

Notice how it wouldn't matter if we paid $10 to get 100 people to look at our sales page or if we got 5,000 people to look at it. What matters is how many became a paying customer and how much it cost to get them.

Easy peasy...

## 7. COST PER LEAD

**Abbreviation:** *CPL*
**Calculation:** *The cost to get someone to opt-in*

This is another pretty simple calculation that you'll use often as an online marketer. Building an email list is elementary. You pretty-much have to do it to be successful in this business. So, this is a good place to start.

At some point in your career, you're likely going to build a squeeze page—a free offer page where you give something valuable in exchange for a prospect's email address.

In the process, their email address is added to your list and you're free to send them content and offers until they opt-out.

There are a number of ways to get people to your squeeze page such as running ads on web sites, buying solo ads (paying someone with a large email list send out your free offer), and a lot more.

Although you're giving away something free, the real purpose of a squeeze page is to get them on your mailing list so you can sell them something down the road.

One thing you *must* do is calculate how much it costs to gain a lead. Eventually, when they do make a purchase, you can use this cost to calculate your real profit. If you sell something for $10 but it cost you $12 to get the lead, you *might* want to look for cheaper ways to get leads (not necessarily, though, as you'll see in a later section).

Here's how it works: Let's say you built a squeeze page for a free PDF eBook. All a visitor has to do to receive the eBook is enter their email address and hit the submit button. When they do, your autoresponder will automatically add them to your email list and send them a download link.

But, what did it cost to get them on your list? Let's say you ran an ad to your squeeze page at 10-cents a click. So, for 100 people to see your page, it cost you $10. If after visiting your page 40-people opted-in, your *Cost per Lead* (CPL) would be:

$10 divided by 40 = 25-cents per lead.

That is *really* cheap lead generation and I would call that a big success in most circumstances. However, keep in mind it's only a hypothetical example and it might prove difficult to achieve in the real world, but it's definitely possible.

Anyway, you see how simple it is to calculate your Cost per Lead? You just take how much it cost to get people to your squeeze page and divide it by the number of people that successfully opted-in. Simple.

Moving on…

## 8. VISITOR VALUE

**Abbreviation:** *VV*

**Calculation:** *Total profit divided by Number of Visitors*

Although this is a simple calculation, the concept behind it is extremely difficult for a lot of people to accept. It's been my experience that some people will *never* understand this concept, but those that do will be far better marketers.

The reason for this difficulty is that I'm going to have you assign a value figure to visitors that spend no money at all. I'm talking about a specific dollar amount that *actually puts real money* into your pocket even though that visitor never made any transaction in the real world.

Confused? I'll bet. Anyway, I'm going to do my best to explain it and hope you "get" it. Those of you that understand "mathematical expectancy" or if you're a scientific poker player familiar with EV (expected value) then you'll be way ahead of the rest.

But, I'm most excited for those of you who haven't been exposed to any of this stuff before. If you can get this one concept, you'll feel like you can see the invisible.

Not only that, but the next two calculations build on this concept and can completely change the way you strategize your business.

Right about now I'm guessing some of you are really excited to learn what I'm about to teach you, while others are scared to death. I'm also guessing a few of you are wondering if you bought a book written by a lunatic.

Never fear… the calculation is extremely simple and all of you will be able to use it in your marketing career. It's the esoteric concept behind it that I'll probably lose a few of you over. Anyway, let's get to it.

As the heading of this section indicates, the calculation is *Visitor Value* (VV). Here's how to calculate it:

Take the profit you made for a given number of visitors then divide that profit by the number of visitors.

For example, let's say you sent 100 visitors to your sales page and two of them made the purchase. Again, we will use our eBook with a CTO of $6.14, so that means we profited a total of $12.28.

So, at a total profit of $12.28 divided by 100 total visitors = .1228 or approximately 12.3-cents per visitor.

Now here's the tricky part. When you make a sale in this situation, you need to think of the visitor that made the purchase as someone that made you 12.3-cents, not someone that made a $6.14 purchase.

But, still harder to visualize is the fact that you should also think of visitors that didn't purchase anything as visitors that made you 12.3-cents as well!

Your Visitor Value is 12.3-cents no matter if they buy anything or not.

What's great about thinking in these terms is that you now have a number to shoot for when you buy advertising. You'll need to get clicks to your web site for under 12.3-cents per click to at least break even. There's no more guessing. That's the number.

That's not to say your Visitor Value won't continually change as you target different groups, etc., but now you have a solid number to work with.

OK, I think everyone probably understands the concept I'm trying to teach here. After all, it's a pretty straightforward and simple calculation. But, as you'll see as we cover the next two calculations, your Visitor Value has other factors affecting the final tally.

## 9. CUSTOMER VALUE

**Abbreviation:** *CV*

**Calculation:** *(Product + Upsells) divided by Total Customers*

Once we have some customers, it's time to assign a value to them. Now, if all you have is a single PDF eBook and two people purchased, then it would seem it's a simple matter of adding up the two CTO totals and dividing by two to get your *Customer Value* (CV). However, it doesn't necessarily work that way.

The difference is when you have an upsell. Let's say we are selling our $7 eBook with a CTO of $6.14, but when the customer makes the purchase, they are taken to an upsell offer for a $27 video package. Now, they don't have to make this purchase, but if they do, it is added to their checkout total.

I'm not going to break down the CTO calculation of the $27 product here in detail, but let's say it comes out to $24.56 (should be pretty close).

let's also say one of our customers takes the upsell and our total for everything comes out to: $6.14 x 2 = $12.28 + $24.56 = $36.84.

So, now, what's our Customer Value? Well, we sold 2 eBooks and one upsell for a total of $36.84 and there were two customers involved so:

$36.84 divided by 2 = $18.42

We are averaging $18.42 per customer. Customer Value = $18.42

Now, so far we've only made two transactions and that's not really enough to boldly say we know our precise Customer Value on this project. But, we have to go with what we have to work with and as more and more transactions take place, our Customer Value will get closer to an accurate number.

But, with the addition of the upsell, something else has happened here. Not only has our Customer Value increased, but we now have to go back and readjust the **<u>Visitor</u>** *Value* we did previously.

If you remember, our *Visitor Value* in the previous section came out to 12.3-cents per visitor. But that was because we sold two eBooks with a total CTO of $12.28. But, now, we bring an upsell into the mix and our CTO is $36.84!

So, for 100 visitors and a total of 2 sales with one upsell our Visitor Value comes out to:

$36.84 divided by 100 = approximately 36.8-cents

With the addition of the upsell, our Visitor Value has more than doubled! We can now increase our ad spend up to 36-cents a click and still do OK. Not that we want to spend more money per click, but our options have opened up for additional opportunities and more opportunities means more ways to make money.

If this section was a little confusing, go through it a couple more times and you'll get it. Next, we're going to confuse it even more with *Customer Lifetime Value* and that one will provoke yet another readjustment to both Visitor Value and Customer Value. Yikes!

But, I have full confidence that you'll master it all in no time. Remember, the calculations themselves are simple; it's the concepts behind them that can sometimes be confusing.

## 10. CUSTOMER LIFETIME VALUE

**Abbreviation:** *CLV*

**Calculation:** *Average profit you can expect for each customer over the duration*

Note: this calculation is also known as *Lifetime Customer Value*. It doesn't matter which way you go: CLV or LCV. It's the same thing, so don't get wrapped up in it. I chose CLV because a lot of the original direct mail gurus I studied 30-years ago called it that. Call me a traditionalist.

We're about to calculate *Customer Lifetime Value* (CLV). If you get to the point where you're using this calculation on a regular basis it probably means you have fully arrived as a pro online marketer.

As you'll see, there's a lot of magic happening within this calculation. For one thing, you'll be running campaigns that to an outsider seem crazy.

Let me give you an example. I'm sure you've probably seen commercials for the *Icy Hot patch* for pain relief. Anyway, when the original company started it was selling the Icy Hot medication as an analgesic balm you rubbed on your joints or arms and it treated arthritis, bursitis pain, muscle strain, etc.

They sold it only through mail order at the time and the product sold for $3 per jar. It was a great product and those that tried it loved it. The problem was the company had no advertising budget.

But, the owner of the company did something smart: He hired well-known marketing genius, Jay Abraham, to help out.

What Jay did was utilize the power of Customer Lifetime Value. Since there was no advertising budget, he suggested that instead of paying for advertising, they would pay for customers and results.

They went to radio stations, TV stations, newspapers, and other media, but didn't pay for advertising. Instead they said, "If you want to sell this product for $3, you can keep 100%." Of course, the media outlets thought they were insane, but loved the idea and took them up on it.

The result was that in 18-months *Icy Hot* went from a little $20,000 a year company to making $13-million. Ultimately, the company sold out to a large pharmaceutical company for a king's ransom.

The success for Icy Hot was all due to Customer Lifetime Value. Remember, they gave up 100% of the selling price for the product and even lost money because they had to manufacture and ship it. Yet, they somehow ended up making $13-million in 18-months. How was this possible?

I'll give you the details in a bit, but right now let me show you how CLV works.

When you calculate CLV you consider not only the total profit you make from each customer with your product and all the upsells, but also the average profit you make on all future purchases for the *lifetime* of that customer.

This means if you acquire a new customer, you would not calculate CLV until many months, or even a few years into the future after they've had a chance to purchase more products and services from your company.

Let's say we're selling our $7 eBook with a CTO of $6.14 as well as the $27 upsell with a CTO of $24.56.

But, let's say over the course of the next two years we sent out emails promoting other products and services—not only for our own products, but also those in which we receive affiliate commissions—and the average customer buys a total of $270 in CTO.

So, in this case, the average customer has a CLV (Customer Lifetime Value) of $135 per year. That's because we ran our stats for two years at $270 so divide that by two and we get $135 per year.

Now, in essence, we could easily spend $200 to acquire a customer because we know we will get $270 back over the course of two years. Personally, I like to average it out on a yearly basis. But, that's just me. You could in fact extend it out to however long you feel comfortable as long as you factor in *attrition* (the average length of time a customer remains a customer before they fade away due to loss of interest or whatever).

But, think about this for a minute. What I'm saying here is that after you have enough data to prove the numbers, you could spend $8 to sell a $7 eBook without batting an eye… and, your business would be *way* profitable at the end of the year! Isn't that insane?

To someone that doesn't know what's going on here it looks like you're a crazy fool and they wonder where you get all your money.

Now that you know the magic of Customer Lifetime Value, let's look back at the *Icy Hot* example. Remember they were letting advertisers keep 100% of the sale.

The product was selling for $3 per jar, but the cost to manufacture and ship was only 45-cents (in the 1970s). In addition, 70% of customers that tried it reordered an average of 6-times a year. So, that meant, in total, 70% of customers spent an additional $18 a year pretty much for as long as they had pain or died, or whatever.

So, let's do a little math and see what happened. On average, out of 100 customers, 70 of them spend $18 per year after the initial sale. That means 70 x $18 = $1,260

But, it also cost 45-cents to manufacture and ship every order, so we need to deduct that from the profit.

.45 x 100 = $45.00 for the initial sale plus 70 x .45 = $31.50 x 6 = $189.00 for the 6 reorders. So, $45 + $189 = $234 total costs.

They brought in $1,260 at a cost of $234 so the total CTO is $1,026 for 100 total customers ($1,260 - $234 = $1,026).

In the end Icy Hot made an average of $10.26 per customer per year for *giving away* that first sale ($1,026 divided by 100).

As you can see, marketing math allows you to see what's really happening below the surface. Once you master Customer Lifetime Value you'll have a whole new outlook on how to make money online. It will be easier to make money because you'll see a whole slew of new options available that the average online marketer will never discover.

## The Secret behind the "Free Book" Giveaways

At the time I first wrote this section, it was popular in the online marketing world to give away a free physical book in exchange for your email. Most of the time, they charge you shipping costs that are obviously too high in order to help cover the cost of the book.

Sometimes, however, they're 100% free including shipping. Now, I don't know exactly how much it costs to produce and ship a 250-page book, but it has to be at least $3 or $4 to have the book printed (in quantity) and another $2.50 to ship it in the U.S. So, using $4 as the printing costs, that's a total of $6.50 per shipment.

So, right away you can see why most of the time they charge you $8.99 to ship you your free book (in that example the marketer would make $2.49 profit for each free book they "give away").

Personally, I don't think they're fooling anyone with the exorbitant "shipping costs." People know the marketer is profiting from the situation. However, I'll bet people order more books under that scenario than if they had said "Get this book for $4 and pay only $2.50 for shipping.

Even though that last idea would be $2.49 less, the "Free Book" + $8.99 shipping wins out because people like "Free Stuff" even if it costs more. That's why testing is so important in online marketing (or, marketing in general).

But, we were examining the 100% free scenario where you get a free book in exchange for your email. Again, this possible because of testing. You have to test in order to calculate true profits.

The marketers giving away 100% free books have tested the situation and utilized the power of Customer Lifetime Value.

If you order one of these 100% free books you will notice you are immediately pummeled with several offers before you even finish your free book order.

They usually start with a rather large offer of about $2,500 or so for some advanced training, and when you don't take that one, they come at you with a $499 offer, then a $270 offer and so on all the way down to a... wait for it... $8.99 offer.

Now, yes, most people reject all of these offers, but enough of them order something along the way and in the end the marketer makes money.

Even if almost everyone passes on all the offers and this campaign loses money the marketer has your email address and isn't finished selling you stuff.

A lot of the marketers giving away free stuff are millionaires because they test and understand the power of Customer Lifetime Value.

And, now, you do too.

SECTION THREE

**PREDICTABLE MONTHLY INCOME**

# THE PLAN FOR MONTHLY INCOME

Now that you've been duly introduced to the mathematical side of positive cash flow, it's time to cut to the chase… to reduce your scrambled ideas of how online marketing works into something simple and beautiful.

Making money online is simple. The problem, though, is everyone tries to make it complicated. Most new online marketers spend their time looking for opportunities to make money. They say, "I just need one super-awesome way to make money online to get started."

That's a dangerous way to go about it because it provokes Shiny Object Syndrome. What will happen is you'll end up searching for anything and everything that might make you some money and before you know it you've got a hard drive full of ideas.

In this business you don't need more ideas, you need focus and direction. Rather than just looking for an idea you hope will work, I want you to ask yourself the following question:

What would be a reasonable amount of money to

make per month through online marketing?

It's important to ask yourself this question and put a number on it. What would be an acceptable amount of money to bring-in per month through online marketing? If you're just starting out, perhaps it's only $100. Start small for the first month, if you hit that number you can always increase it next month.

Usually, when I ask someone how much money they want to make each month they say, "As much as possible." Well, "as much as possible" isn't a number. When you answer it like that you end up spending your time looking for opportunities and collecting more and more *shiny objects*.

Stop doing that right now or you'll never make it as an online marketer!

The reason you need to put a number on it isn't just so you can prove you can reach your goal, it's because once you have a solid number to work with you can formulate a *plan*. You'll have direction and focus and that, my friends, is half the battle.

## How To Formulate Your Plan For Positive Cash Flow

Let's say you set your monthly income goal at $300. To achieve this, the first step is to break it down into a daily quota. On average, there are 30.42 days in a month. I arrived at that number by taking the number of days in a year (365) and dividing it by 12 months. 365/12 = 30.416667 or, 30.42 after rounding off.

In order to make $300 a month our daily quota breaks down as follows:

$300/30.42 = $9.86

So, you'll need to make $9.86 every day to hit your goal of $300 a month. The beauty of this—and, the life changing part—is you're no longer wandering around trying to make "as much money as possible." Now, you can focus your attention on formulating a plan that gets you that $9.86 a day.

Right away let's come up with a realistic plan to achieve this goal. You already learned that a $7 eBook will have a CTO of $6.14, so let's use that.

In order to make $9.86 we would need to sell $9.86/$6.14 = 1.61 units. That's less than 2-eBooks a day. Not out of the question, right?

But, even better, let's look at how our focus has changed:

We're no longer trying to "make as much money as possible."

We're not trying to make $300 a month.

We're not even trying to make $9.86 a day...

WE'RE FOCUSING ON SELLING AN AVERAGE OF 1.61 EBOOKS A DAY.

1.61 is a simple, doable number. It makes your online life easy. 1.61. That's it.

Heck, you could probably put up a few fliers on telephone poles to get that kind of action.

But, what if later on we need more money? What if we need to pay all our bills and feed our family?

It's the same thing, only bigger...

Let's say we need to come up with $4,103 every month as a bare minimum to survive. It's probably safe to say you're not going to get there with a single $7 eBook to sell, but just for the sake of argument, let's run the numbers and see what would happen if we tried it that way:

Our $7 product has a CTO of $6.14. So, how many of those babies would we have to sell every day to make our $4,103 monthly expenses?

$4,103 divided by $6.14 = 668.24 divided by 30.42 = 21.97

So, if you're going to go with a single $7 product you'll need to sell about 22 of them a day.

Now, I'm not saying it's impossible to make $4,103 a month selling a $7 product, but that's probably not realistic unless you consider things like list building and lots of affiliate sales along with it.

But, that's why we do this exercise in the first place... to formulate a plan. We can see after running a few numbers that trying to make this kind of monthly income right away with a single $7 eBook probably isn't going to work.

Let's try a different idea. How about a $97 product with a CTO of $84.39?

How many units would we have to sell each month to make our expenses, then?

Let's see... $4,103 divided by $84.39 = 48.62

So, we need to sell about 49 units every month to make our expenses. This actually looks like a doable scenario as long as the product is good and the market is healthy enough to support that many sales.

Breaking down further...

365 days in a year divided by 12 months = 30.42

So, if we need to sell 49 units a month we have to

divide that by 30.42 days and we get: 1.61 (it's a coincidence that the number is 1.61 again, I should re-do it to avoid confusion, but I'm not).

Again, all we have to do to make our $4,103 expenses is sell 1.61 units a day.

Isn't online marketing awesome?

Try this yourself with different combinations of products. You could start with a $7 PDF eBook as a tripwire and upsell to a $47 instructional video and then upsell once more to a $197-per-month group coaching program. The possibilities are endless.

Anyhow, I don't want to get into a multitude of scenarios here in this section; I just want to express the need to have a monthly number so you can realistically design your online marketing plan to fit your personal situation.

Calculate your monthly number then figure out how to get it; don't just start selling stuff. Have purpose behind everything you do and you'll treat it more as a business. This is where success online begins.

Do this before you even create a product!

Seriously, you won't know what you'll need to create in terms of products until you know what you're going to need in terms of monthly income.

And, speaking of products...

# PRO-LEVEL PRODUCT CREATION

In the previous section I assumed you would be creating your own product to sell. If you're going to be a pro in the online marketing business you definitely need something to sell and preferably it should be something that originates from you.

It's not that you can't make a lot of money promoting other people's products, but contrary to what most newbies think, it's a lot harder to be successful that way. At the very least you should have a low ticket product to use for list building.

Anyway, if you're not the product creation type there's another option. You could always hire someone to create a product for you. Fortunately for me, I have a knack for creating unique products out of thin air (seriously, have you ever read anything like the book you're reading right now?) but, if I was going to have a product created for me, here's how I would do it:

## How To Work With An Outsourcer

First of all, I'd gather as much up-to-date information

as I could on a specific subject. I'd buy all the latest books and eBooks and start going through them one-by-one to extract the best parts. I would get to know the subject really well until I came up with some unique ideas of my own to enhance the extracted information. This is critical! You *must* add something new to the mix or it's just going to be rehashed junk.

Next, I would compile my notes and create an outline of what the product would look like. Then, I would seek out someone to create the product based on that outline, my notes, and the gathered information.

Make sure you mark the portions of your notes and the gathered information as "You can use this 'as written' if needed" and "COPIED INFORMATION: MUST BE COMPLETELY REWRITTEN." This is important! You don't want a plagiarism suit on your hands.

You can find ghost writers on websites such as Upwork or Warrior Forum to write your report. It's going to cost you anywhere from $80 to $500 for a well-written 20-page report to get you started. Make sure you get some samples of their work before you hire someone.

After I got the finished report back I would go through it and find everything that needs to be rewritten then send it back to the writer for editing. When I got the final edits back *I would completely rewrite the whole report!*

I know, it seems stupid to pay someone to create a product for you and then you completely rewrite it, but that's how I'd do it. I want my products to be a reflection of who I am as much as possible, so I have to put as much of me into it as possible.

I'm guessing some of you are probably thinking, if I'm

just going to rewrite it anyway, why not buy some cheap, $1.50 PLR instead of forking out big bucks for a ghost writer?

I don't recommend purchasing PLR products because they are almost always crap. Not just crap, but *unusable-in-any-way* crap. Seriously, I've never seen *cheap* PLR you could ever use other than maybe the cover art.

Most of the PLR I've seen—even most of the more expensive stuff—is just words on paper to take up space. I've rarely seen anything that teaches anything useful; if it does, it's usually so out-of-date and obsolete it's worthless.

Please resist the urge to go cheap. If you're going to put your name on it, at least make sure the final product is something you can be proud of.

## Doing It Yourself

If you think you can skip the ghost writer and do it all yourself you basically follow the same game plan as above:

1. Gather up-to-date information
2. Buy the latest books and digital products on the topic and extract the best info
3. Add your own ideas
4. Create an outline
5. Create a product based on that outline

Simple, right?

Anyway, that's how you do it.

## Creating Videos And Audios

Another option is to create a video or audio. In a lot of ways, this is even simpler than writing an eBook. I would still follow the 5-steps as I explained above, only instead of putting it on paper; I'd just build it into a PowerPoint style presentation or, even easier, read it into a recorder to produce an audio product.

One thing's for sure, if you do an audio it's a much faster process. You could easily do your product in an hour. However, people don't seem to perceive audios to be as valuable as video or even eBooks.

Still, there's a ton of money to be made doing audios. I know of one very successful online marketer that almost exclusively utilizes audio for his products. The guy makes—according to him—around $20,000 per month doing that.

Now, that's not *all* from audio. He uses the audio sales to funnel people into his live group coaching program or to upsell them to higher-ticket products (usually consisting of more audios—some of which are the recordings from his coaching calls!).

Anyway, there are a lot of benefits to doing audios. Think about this: you could easily do one or two audios a week and by the end of the year you'd have 50-100 finished products!

I'll bet that's more than 95% of the people who read this book.

## Guru Trick To Instantly Increase Perceived Value

As I mentioned, audios are the simplest and fastest

form of product creation, but they lack the perceived value of video. So, why not take 10-minutes and turn them into videos?

This is so simple, it's criminal. There's two ways to do this:

The first way is to create a title slide and set your screen capture software to show only that while you record audio. When you're done, you're done.

Yes, I'm saying *just* a title slide; no presentation whatsoever.

Another way is to record your audio and then create a title slide and meld them together into a video with a video editing application. This is how you'll have to do it if you already have audios or if you record a phone conversation or live interview.

Now, there's one thing you must do if you follow this advice. If you're creating videos from audios and the only on-screen image is the title slide, it must be made clear these are "simple videos."

In other words, when you sell a product like this you must give some indication they aren't detailed screen capture instructional videos or people will feel cheated. What I normally do is phrase it like this on my sales page:

"Get these 6-simple videos explaining... blah, blah, blah..."

I can't stress enough the importance of keeping everything above board. It's your reputation that's at stake and it's never a good idea to mislead anyone for a few extra sales.

## Take It To An Even Higher Level

If you follow my advice above on how to increase the value of your audios by turning them into simple videos you're probably going to have some "winners" and some "losers."

The good news is, even though the greater majority of them will be "losers," the time you put into creating them is only a fraction of what you'd put into more difficult-to-produce products like eBooks.

But, the even better news is after you start making some sales, you're going to see what types of information people want and are more willing to pay for.

This information is *pure gold!*

For every ten-or-so audios you produce you're going to hit one or two winners. If you want to really blow up your bank account I suggest you take the winning products—those which have already proven to make sales—and spend time turning those into more sophisticated products.

The easiest way to do that is to go back and add a full-blown PowerPoint style presentation to go along with the audio you've already created. If you do only this one thing you can realistically charge at least 3-times what you were originally selling it for as an audio or simple video.

Add a downloadable PDF document or two (even if it's only a transcript and/or checklist) to the package and you can charge even more. What's great about this product updating technique is you're not spending a bunch of time creating all this stuff for products that aren't going to sell.

Use your simple audios as a testing ground to weed out the duds and expand the winners!

Is this Red-Pill Matrix stuff, or what? ☺

# INSTANT CREDIBILITY

Credibility is one of the most valuable assets a digital marketer can possess. But, unless you have some way to prove you're credible, most people automatically assume you're just some "internet guy" (or gal) who's there to take advantage of them.

That's because people who buy digital products have been burned so many times they've become jaded. Even those who've never made an online purchase have heard stories and are skeptical as well.

The unfortunate truth is a large section of the online marketing community has become filled with people selling over-hyped garbage that leads to disappointment.

They're in it for the money (see *The Big Secret* chapter).

It's no wonder potential customers are skeptical.

But, what if you were different? What if you were able to stand out from the crowd and somehow produce an instant aura of credibility to *everyone*... including those who've never heard of you before?

Well, it's possible, and that's what I'm going to show you in this chapter.

## Promise Me You Won't Freak Out...

What I'm about to show you is going to scare a lot of people, but please stick with me and read the entire section; there's going to be a lot about the psychology of sales in here that will be of benefit to you, even if you flat-out refuse to follow my advice.

Now, of course, not everything I'm about to show you will lead to stark terror; but, I wanted to prepare you for the parts of it that several surveys rank as *even more terrifying than dying*!

Yup... as you may have guessed, I'm talking about public speaking. Now, wait! Remember, you promised you weren't going to freak out!

I'm *not* going to recommend you get up on a stage and deliver a presentation to a room full of online gurus or anything like that (although, that would be a *great* way to gain instant credibility).

In fact, most of what I'm going to show you will not necessarily result in you having to perform live or communicate with anyone. But, it *could*.

## Working Without A Net

The more credibility you can produce the more you'll get people to trust you and if they trust you, they'll be much more willing to buy from you or follow your recommendations.

Let's say you put out a PDF eBook as a WSO on the

Warrior Forum and it sold pretty well. Let's also say you got a few really good reviews.

Everything is going great.

But, then you get an email from one of your customers who asks, "Hey, would you be willing to get on the phone with me to answer a few related questions that weren't covered in your eBook?"

Maybe they further explain they would be willing to PayPal you $10 if you'd give them 15-minutes of your time.

Would you do it?

It's one thing to spend a few days polishing up an eBook so you look like you know what you're talking about, and quite another to answer random, unknown questions on the fly.

You might start wondering if you know your subject well enough to pull it off without embarrassment. What if there's a question you can't answer and you look like a fraud?

Believe me; this will go through your mind the first time it happens to you.

But, your decision to do the call or not says a lot about your credibility. You could respond with, "Sorry, I don't do consults." And, as long as the customer doesn't go blabbing about it all over the internet, you've kept the situation private and it might not impact your credibility too much.

However, by taking the "safe" route you're missing a golden opportunity. If you're smart, and can muster up just a little bit of courage, you can leverage this simple situation into something much bigger.

Not only can you increase your credibility in the eyes

of this one customer *and* the rest of the online community, but you can also use it to *instantly increase the value of your product* and make more sales.

Instead of just doing the call, satisfying this one customer and pocketing a measly $10, you could offer to do the call for free under the condition that he lets you record the call and add the resulting recording to your product.

Now, assuming you did the call and everything went well, look at what you've got:

1. You've satisfied this customer.

2. You've increased the value of your product by including the recording.

But, most importantly:

3. You've potentially increased your *overall credibility* by demonstrating you're enough of an expert to answer questions live.

This single act of "doing it live," even though it was only in the presence of one person, has magnified your credibility to anyone who sees the sales letter for your eBook with the inclusion of a bonus recording: *a live coaching call explaining important related details*.

By demonstrating you're willing to "work without a net" and answer live questions, takes you out of the potential *online charlatan* column and puts you into the *online expert* column.

There's no way to fake it when you do it live. And, that's what makes this such an excellent way to establish instant credibility. Everyone knows you have to be an expert to do it.

## The Power Of Live Webinars

OK, WAIT!

I can sense the average reader of this book clutching at their heart and hyperventilating...

But, remember, we promised not to freak out...

Besides, if you were willing to do the phone call, it's really only a hop-skip-and-a-jump to do a live webinar.

In fact, in many ways a live webinar requires LESS expertise than a 1-on-1 coaching call. That's because you get to *pre-determine* the topics you'll cover and *you get to choose which questions to answer*!

During the course of a live webinar, it's true you are usually pummeled with dozens of questions. But, these questions are normally hidden from the attendees and you can simply postpone answering any questions you can't figure-out at the moment. You can always say, "Jack, I see your question and I'll have to get back to you on that one..."

Just make sure you make a note and really do follow up with Jack later on after you've done some research.

Anyway, doing webinars is almost a requirement these days; or, at least if you want to make big bucks, it is.

If you don't believe me, try to think of a big-name guru who doesn't periodically do webinars or at least some kind of live training or coaching.

You can't! There is no such thing!

That's because there's no way to demonstrate you're an expert without being willing to work without a net on some level—and nothing beats webinars for doing just that.

## The Live Coaching Option

If you haven't had much experience interacting live, the thought of live coaching probably makes you even more nervous than the webinar idea; however, by setting up a live coaching program, you're able to benefit just by the fact you're willing to offer it in the first place, even if you never end up coaching anyone.

Let me explain...

Let's say someone visits your website and sees you have an interesting product for sale. It looks like something they might want, but they don't know much about you so they take a few minutes to look at your website.

Now, if they see you also offer 1-on-1 live coaching, wouldn't that increase your credibility in their eyes?

They still don't know you and are unlikely to take you up on your offer for coaching, but after seeing you did make the offer, they almost *have* to believe you know more than the average product creator to offer such a program.

So, they go back to the original product they were looking at and buy it because now they have a good indication you're not some faker.

The psychological impact and the reasoning produced will have them believe the product you're selling is more likely to deliver on its promises since it's from someone who's obviously expert enough to also offer a live, 1-on-1 coaching program.

See how that works?

It's the willingness to work without a net that does it.

ALL your products become instantly more valuable in the eyes of potential customers by virtue of the coaching offer. *Even if no one ever takes you up on it!*

## The Live Coaching Gambit

The response I most often get from newbies when I suggest they offer a coaching program is, "But, William, I'm not ready to offer a coaching program!"

Oh, really? Well, if you know enough to put up a website and add a contact form to apply to your coaching program, you're ahead of anyone that doesn't have a clue how to do those things.

Also, I'm sure there are other things you know that others need help with.

But, I understand where you're coming from; maybe you're one of those people who freeze up at any human interaction or you just don't yet feel comfortable enough with your abilities to charge for coaching services.

If you're a complete newbie, you probably *shouldn't* offer a coaching program at all.

All of that is OK and I wouldn't offer a coaching program if you're just not ready.

But, here's the truth:

No one is ever going to seek coaching from you if you haven't already proven to them you have something of value to offer.

In other words, if they haven't already bought a product from you or experienced your knowledge in some way, there is almost no chance they are going to contact you for high-priced coaching.

If you're new, you'll have enough trouble getting someone to spend $7 for your eBook.

What I'm getting at here is—in most cases—you can safely offer a coaching program and gain the valuable credibility it delivers without fear of actually having to coach anyone.

But, you may be thinking, what if someone *does* contact me for coaching?

Well, in the highly unlikely event that does happen and you don't think you're capable of helping them, you can always tell them you don't currently have any openings for new coaching clients or just offer to put them on a waiting list.

A waiting list is pretty common anyway especially for live group coaching programs because you need to gather enough clients to make it worth your while. You don't want to start group training with only one or two people and then have others join after the training has already been going on for 6-weeks.

Of course, I recommend you actually *do* follow through and create a coaching program because that's where the real money is in online marketing.

Besides, getting started as a coach isn't as difficult as you'd think. It's not really necessary to pre-plan several weeks of coaching lessons; some of the best coaching advice I ever got was to not try and put together a planned course and just wing-it instead.

Why? Because you'll find nearly 100% of the time you'll have to change direction anyway due to the needs of your clients.

Let their needs determine the next steps in your coaching lessons.

## For The Brave With Experience...

Now, if you do have a lot of experience and are brave enough to do it, I've got to say there are few things more profitable than taking on live coaching clients.

If this is you then you should follow a more proactive strategy for getting clients than just putting a contact form on your website.

One way to do that is to offer free, 30-minute phone or Skype conversations with promising clients.

You might want to make it clear you don't work with start-ups or people in idea phase. You only want to work with people who are already making sales.

These are the types of people who just need some guidance on sales funnels, increasing conversions, etc.

The reason you don't want to work with start-ups and other non-successful clients is because for the most part they are functioning off of a dream. They won't have money to pay you and all you'll be doing is wasting your time.

Once you do get a good potential client on a call, it's your job to listen to their situation and try to come up with two or three actionable strategies to execute.

You hold nothing back. You give them the best possible advice you can. You want to prove you can help them.

YOU DON'T ASK THEM FOR MONEY!

If you did your job correctly and gave them some truly helpful and actionable information, they will very often ask if they can hire you right there on the call.

If not, and you sense they are almost there, you can ask the standard pro-coaching question: "Would you like help with that going forward?"

If they say, "Yes," then you can explain your terms: "The way this works is, I offer weekly 30-minute coaching calls for $500 per month." Or, whatever your rates are.

Note you are not offering to do the actual work for them, you are a business coach and it's your job to help them with business *strategy*. You're not a tech support or website builder.

What if they don't seem like they're interested in moving forward with you?

Then, simply wish them good luck and hope they let others know how helpful you've been.

Just move on to the next one.

## Group Coaching

If you're already selling products a great upsell is group coaching.

For example, if you're selling a $97 course on writing a first novel, you can upsell a by-weekly live group coaching call for $27-a-month.

All you do is take questions from your students and answer them live on a webinar twice a month.

If you get 100 people to take that upsell, that's an extra $2,700 a month for just a couple hours of your time.

And, 100 participants on a webinar is usually not too many to handle; many of the questions they have will be common questions that get answered collectively. So, there's literally zero chance you'll get bombarded with

100 separate and unique questions.

Normally, with only 100 participants you'll find it difficult to get enough questions to fill the allotted time.

**Final Thoughts On Credibility**

The most important thing you can take away from this chapter is you need to develop a willingness to work without a net.

As I explained early on in this book, your overall philosophy should be to try and help people solve problems, and by-far the best way to do that is to help them in real time. Get on the phone with them or do webinars.

Show the people in your niche you're the expert and, to prove it, you're willing and capable of answering their questions live.

Competitors who refuse to do this will be left in the dust.

## GETTING THINGS DONE

If you have no problem putting together a product and getting it out there for sale, you definitely don't need to read any further, you probably just need to re-read the chapter titled "The Big Secret" to help you readjust your online marketing philosophy.

However, if you're like I was before I stumbled onto this final concept, you already know what you need to do, but for some reason you can't seem to make it happen.

If that's you, then this is going to make all the difference.

Here's what I want you to do:

***Allow yourself to make mistakes.***

That's right, make mistakes. The more mistakes the better.

Why? Because it's impossible to go from where you are now to where you want to be without making mistakes along the way.

It only stands to reason that the faster you get those mistakes out of the way the faster you'll reach your goals.

People think of mistakes as something to avoid; and, sure, if you see them coming, by all means avoid them. They're bad.

But, you know what's even worse? To let the mere *possibility* of mistakes turn you into a non-productive loser.

If you're constantly stopping to evaluate the potential for making a mistake, you're unnecessarily adding time to your projects.

Think about it... every time you try to work on your project, you hesitate because the voice in your head says it's not good enough or it looks amateurish or this could never work or it's not grammatically correct or no one is going to want to buy this, etc.

I could list a thousand reasons why you can't get going, but the real reason—the root of your problem—is that you're afraid to make a mistake.

So, from now on, do what I've learned to do: Plow through and fix the mistakes later.

If you're writing something, write crap and fix it later. Use a little *ABT* (always be typing).

If you write 500-words of crap, you'll discover 100 of them are pretty good and can be used without too much editing.

100-words are better than none, right?

The best part is, after you get used to doing things this way, you'll start to trust yourself and see a significant improvement on the quality of your writing and you'll get much more than just 100 good words.

You'll eventually get to where almost everything you write is usable except for a little polishing. That's when you'll really start producing.

And, it works on *everything*, not just writing projects.

If you're shooting a screen-capture video go ahead and start the recording and keep moving. You can always edit it later or at the very least you'll get an idea of what it's like and be able to create a useable "take-2" whereas before you'd be staring at the screen trying to figure out the best way to start.

If you're doing a squeeze page, do it in ten minutes and send traffic to it. If it doesn't work, re-do it. That's better than spending hours wondering if it will work and convincing yourself to keep tweaking it until it "looks good to me."

Heck, you probably won't *ever* think it looks good and end up quitting before you even test it. That happens a lot.

### Allow yourself to make mistakes and keep moving.

As copywriting legend, Gary Halbert used to say, "Momentum, not mediation."

I know of one very well-known online marketer that launches his products with simply horrible looking sales pages. They are riddled with major typos and he does this constantly. I know this guy and how he operates and his sales pages are typo farms because he believes speed is the most important factor in online marketing.

Don't get me wrong; the content of the sales pages are pure genius and sell his products like crazy, but the spelling mistakes and typos are unbelievable.

Most of us would be embarrassed to let the world see something we created looking so awful, but I really don't think he gets embarrassed anymore. Probably because he's made millions online and can always fix things later (most of the time he leaves the typos in there unless it's something confusing to the reader).

The point is, mistakes are fixable and momentum is the key.

**Releasing Into The Wild**

Another major problem you'll come across when you have a fear of mistakes is not being able to finalize your project.

What happens is you're afraid it's not good enough for public consumption and you keep tweaking and tweaking.

Well, I have bad news for you: it's *never going to be good enough!*

If you want to have any chance at success in this business you're going to have to make yourself say "it's good enough" and let it go.

Deep down, I'm a perfectionist. So, what I've had to learn is to get my project about 80% perfect then release it for sale even though it kills me to do so when I think it still needs work.

But, you know what? My customers love my products and, to them, it seems pretty close to perfect as it is.

In a nutshell, here's my process:

Get my product to 80% perfect and release it into the

wild.

After its initial release, I sometimes take the final 20% and get *that portion* to 80% perfect, edit it into my product, and then send an update notification to my customers so they can download the updated version.

After that, unless there are some major changes that need updating, I leave it alone. I'm done with it.

If you find yourself continually tweaking it after that, stop what you're doing and go read Dan Sullivan's *The 80% Approach* instead. ☺

## It's Up To You...

I'm guessing a lot of people will read this chapter and find it worthless, but a handful will consider it one of the most valuable lessons they've ever learned. I hope you fall into the second category.

## SECTION FOUR

# RADIOACTIVE SEEDS

### 16-WAYS TO ENTER THE "MAKE MONEY ONLINE" NICHE WITH YOUR VERY FIRST PRODUCT

(even if you've never made a dime online in your life)

# IMPORTANT NOTES ABOUT THE BONUS SECTION

Most of what you're about to read originally sold online as a $27 PDF eBook called, *Radioactive Seeds: 16-ways to enter the "make money online" niche with your very first product (even if you've never made a dime online in your life).*

I understand this section is not for everyone. You may be in the weight loss niche and have no interest in the "make money online" niche.

However, you might want to read this section anyway because there are plenty of vital lessons helpful to anyone doing online marketing regardless of niche.

Radioactive Seeds has proved to be one of my most popular products, has helped countless online marketers get started in this business, and has the remarkable distinction of being one of the few products that has never received a request for refund.

Now, I rarely get refund requests for my products anyway, but *none*? That's pretty much unheard of in the industry.

I think that says a lot, particularly because it was a

hot seller for years.

Anyway, the reason I'm including a special preface to this bonus section is because I think there are a few things you need to know before you continue.

First of all, up until this point in the book, nearly 100% of the information will remain relevant and unchanged 10-years from now whereas this section will eventually be rendered obsolete.

It might not happen for 5-years or 50, but it's inevitable that at some point the websites and methods I recommend in the following section will change. It's just the nature of the internet.

To reduce this phenomenon, I've removed a lot of the "go here, then click here, then click there," stuff.

It isn't that critical anyway since there's generally instructional videos available on YouTube that walk you through all the important steps. Just do a little creative searching and you'll be good to go.

Also, the content of this section assumes you are a member of the Warrior Forum and understand what I mean by "WSO."

If you have no idea, don't worry, just head over to Warrior Forum and spend some time there. You'll definitely want to join if you have any interest in internet marketing at all. And, it's free to join.

Trust me, everyone that's anyone in this business is, or has been, a member of that forum.

You can get there by going to the following web address:

### http://warriorforum.com

A WSO is a *Warrior Special Offer*. This means that you get a discounted price or something else that makes it special for Warrior Forum members.

I also assume you know about things like autoresponders, list building and the general mechanics of internet marketing. If not, head over to the Warrior Forum and start studying!

Although I highly recommend you start out the WSO route, I want to make it clear that there's nothing that says you *have* to start out that way. You could easily apply the lessons in this section to any selling method you prefer. You could simply create your product and set it up for sale on your own website and completely bypass the Warrior Forum altogether.

However, by doing that you'll miss out on all the super-targeted traffic that comes with posting on the Warrior Forum. But, it's your choice.

It's interesting to note that what you're about to read in this section started out as a WSO. In fact, it was my very first "make money online" product.

As time went on, it gradually evolved into what you see here today.

Enjoy!

# WELCOME TO THE "MAKE MONEY ONLINE" NICHE

I think I know who you are... you've been hanging around the online marketing scene for months, maybe even years. You've learned a ton about how to make money online and purchased several products.

At some point you've probably looked at an online marketing product and said to yourself, "I already knew all this! I should be the one putting out products and making money!"

But, in order to do that you'd have to convince potential buyers—people who've never heard of you before—that what you're selling has real value. And, having no proof of income or past history makes that next to impossible.

So, how do you get around this? Why would anyone take you seriously when you've never made any money online?

That's what this section is all about. I'm going to teach you a product creation concept that will allow you to *legitimately* enter the "online marketing" or "make money online" niches without any authority or proof of income.

Once you create and sell your first product, you *will* have some proof of income and past history to back you up.

Not only that, but you'll finally begin to put together the most important element of online marketing success: an email list.

## Important Disclaimer Info

Please note that the disclaimer at the front of this book titled, "Legal Mumbo-Jumbo," applies to this section as well. Instead of repeating that information here, I will simply make reference to it.

If you need a refresher on what that says, please go re-read that section before you continue.

## THE WORLD'S WORST ONLINE MARKETER

My name is William McCamment and I used to be the WORLD'S WORST ONLINE MARKETER.

It's not because I'm an idiot... I'm at least as smart as the average primate... no, I was the world's worst marketer because I fell for every online money-making system promising days on the beach in your underwear surrounded by gorgeous supermodels bringing you beer.

The truth is, I hardly ever had gorgeous supermodels bringing me beer. Usually, I just sat on the beach in my underwear surrounded by angry policemen.

And, in case you're wondering: Tasers *burn*.

The worst part is... *I knew better!*

None of those crazy online money-making techniques were going to work for very long, if at all.

So, in the bleakest of times... as I sat there in the back of the squad car... my eyes burning from the smoke of my smoldering underpants... I made this critical vow (and so should you):

## *Stop Wasting Time And Money On Promises Of Swashbuckling Adventure And Do Something You <u>ALREADY KNOW</u> Will Work!*

Are you with me?

Good.

So check this out:

If you've spent any time studying online marketing you already know one of the fastest ways to make money is to follow this simple 4-step process:

1. Create a "Make Money Online" Product
2. Sell it to the "Online Marketing" Crowd
3. Build a list of Enthusiastic Buyers
4. Sell more stuff to your list

Simple, right?

But, there's a problem...

You can't just come out and sell your own "make money online" product when you've never made any money online before—even if you've studied online marketing every day for the past five years!

You just wouldn't feel legit and your fellow online marketers would sense it.

What's sad is you probably have more online marketing knowledge than 99% of mainstream product creators out there just by the fact you check out the latest techniques and learn something "online marketing" related every day.

But, the problem with creating your own product in the "make money online" niche is that you haven't put any of that knowledge into practice, so you don't have any personal case studies or proof of income to back up your claims.

So, selling a "make money online" product when you don't have any functional experience is out of the question, right?

Well... not exactly.

## A Clever Solution To The "Credibility" Problem

Right about now you're probably wondering how it's possible for someone with *no track record* to create legitimate products that experienced marketers would not only want to buy, but also be thrilled with the quality of the content.

I know exactly how you feel.

In fact, I felt the same way when I tried to come up with my first "make money online" product.

And, up until a few years ago, I nearly gave up trying to figure it out.

Even my family tried to convince me to "Give up" on this Internet Marketing thing and go get a "real" job.

But then one day something amazing happened: I discovered an interesting loophole to get around this barrier.

It's an ingenious idea for product creation that completely removes the need to prove you're some kind of expert or internet marketing guru... so you don't have to pretend you're something you're not!

Even better, I came up with a system—which I reveal later on in this book—that anyone can use to create these kinds of products.

Look... for a lot of people, it's not even about the money, it's more about showing your friends and family you really can make money online and you're not crazy for refusing to go get a job you're sure to hate.

Here's the way I see it:

Being a full-time internet marketer allows me to...

- **Be my own boss and control my own destiny** – This has always been my biggest beef with working for someone else. You have no control over your own future. In my case, a freak accident (that I was not involved with) forced the company I worked for to close its doors and let all its employees go with no prior warning.

- **Do something I love instead of having every move I make dictated by some knucklehead** – The truth is, I don't take direction well. I really hate being told what to do all the time. I'm sure you do too.

- **Make my own hours** – Don't you hate having to get up and go to work for someone else? I mean, seriously... if you have to get out of bed to help build someone else's dream, doesn't that make you mad? It does me.

- **Be creative** – I'm a naturally creative person and internet marketing allows me to express my creativity. That's a big deal for me.

- **Help people** – I have so many unique solutions and I genuinely love helping people. Internet marketing is a no-brainer profession for this kind of scenario.

If any of that sounds like you, and if you've been an enthusiastic student of online marketing for a while, this bonus section will be right up your alley.

## Time To Get Serious

The goal of this section is to help you finally launch your online marketing career, build a list (of buyers, no less), and effectively shove a sock into the mouths of those who doubt you.

I'm going to show you how it's possible to legitimately enter the "make money online" niche with your very first product.

It shouldn't matter if you've never made money online before because the concepts and product blueprints I provide won't require any proof of income to make sales.

And, I'm even going to prove to you why it's actually *better* to start in this niche than, say… the *Weight Loss* niche.

We've all seen new products explode and make their creators tens of thousands of dollars in a matter of hours. I'm not promising you'll have that kind of success with your first product or that you'll have supermodels feeding you beer on the beach. But, the concepts contained in this book are solid and really could go viral if you put just the right spin on them and market them effectively.

Just remember this: The real purpose of this section

is not to teach you how to make a quick buck or to offer you temporary money-making gimmicks, it's to get you started making sales, building a list and starting a real business online.

# WHY THE "MAKE MONEY ONLINE" NICHE?

I believe the products you create should be based on what you're passionate about. If you spring out of bed every morning excited to start your daily exercise regimen, maybe you should choose the fitness niche; if you can't wait to get off work tonight because your latest beer recipe will finally be ready for consumption, then go into the home-brewing niche. Whatever floats your boat.

But, If you're like me, you love the psychology and mechanics behind online marketing. It's the first thing I think about when I wake up in the morning and it's what I'm thinking about as I fall asleep at night.

Also, starting with a "make money online" product solves a lot of problems. For instance, you won't have to worry about where to find your target market or how you're going to get traffic, all you have to do after you create your product is put it in the WSO section of the Warrior Forum and let it fly. Thousands of *perfectly targeted* customers are already there looking to buy products like yours all day long.

In the pages that follow you'll learn what it takes to enter the online marketing niche with your very first product. It shouldn't matter if you've never created a product or even if you've never made money online before because the methods I recommend won't require any proof of income to make sales.

Look, we're not necessarily going to get rich off this first project, but that's OK. We just need to get started— *a seed*, if you will—something to plant into the online marketing niche in order to grow a full-time business.

I'm calling these types of products *Radioactive Seeds* because, although simple, they could go nuclear at any time without warning. Russ Ruffino's first WSO was only a simple PDF and it reportedly sold $14,000 in a matter of hours.

Obviously, I can't promise you'll have that kind of success with your first project. In fact, some of the blueprints I came up with have nearly no chance of exploding like that. But, some of them really could go viral if you put just the right spin on them and market them effectively. So, who knows?

Just remember this: The goal here is not to make a quick buck, it's to get you started making sales and building a list in the "online marketing" or "make money online" niches.

Where you take it from there is up to you.

## HOW TO SELL TO THE "MAKE MONEY ONLINE" CROWD WHEN YOU'VE NEVER MADE ANY MONEY ONLINE

For the most part, people such as those on the Warrior Forum are there to learn how to make money online. A lot of them get discouraged because they don't see how to legitimately sell a "make money online" product when they've never actually made any money online.

They've purchased enough "make money" products to know the mechanics and methods inside-and-out and feel they could easily teach others, but they've never actually put the methods into practice, so they don't really know firsthand if it even works.

To create and sell a product under these circumstances would be unethical and misleading.

But, there *is* a way to sell to the "make money online" crowd that is both above-board and valuable to those who buy it.

This is great news for those who have never created an internet marketing product because they can now get injected into the "make money online" niche right away and start building a list.

Once you get a list started, you're on your way.

So, how does someone with no track record or proof of income create such a product?

The key is this:

***You <u>can't</u> legitimately show them how to make money, but you <u>can</u> help them to save money or be more efficient.***

If you base your products on this concept, you'll be off and running.

People have a great need to be more efficient and will pay good money if you can save them large chunks of time.

For example, I figure I need to make at least $50-per-hour to do anything internet marketing-related and make it worth my while, so if someone was selling a $7 report explaining how to save four hours doing something I needed to do I'd be stupid not to buy it!

It's a matter of simple math:

**4 hours of my time = $200 (minimum)**
**Report to save 4 hours - $7**
**Total value = $193 or more**

Do you have a way to be more efficient and have the ability to teach others how to do it? Put it into a report or create a video and sell it!

If at all possible, it's a good idea to be crystal clear when explaining the value of saving time in your sales material. Be specific as possible like I did above.

# WHY YOU CAN'T LOSE WITH YOUR FIRST PRODUCT

The beautiful thing about creating your first online marketing product is that, if you do it right, you can't lose with it. Here's what I mean:

If your product sells really well you'll make a lot of money. Nothing wrong with that, right?

But, if your product doesn't sell, or doesn't sell very well you still have options. You can create another product and offer your original product as a bonus. You can use it as a give-away for a squeeze page to build a list. You can use it as a bonus to promote an affiliate product. If you think about it, the possibilities are almost endless.

Whether your first product sells well or not, you should always consider creating future products that are closely related. That way, you'll be able to bundle everything together and sell the resulting collection as a more expensive product with a much higher perceived value.

## Pick Something and Go!

In the next few pages I'm going to give you 16- blueprints (seeds) to get you started in the IM niche.

Maybe you've already thought of something you think will work. If so, go with that. Don't worry about what you're going to add as an OTO or any of that... just pick something and go with it—no upsells unless you've already got one ready. This is your first product, so make it simple and quick. You can always add to it later if you want.

For those that need a kick-start, here are 16 blueprints you can use for product creation that have already been done and have proven to be successful.

## 16 PRODUCT BLUEPRINTS YOU CAN USE TO START YOUR ONLINE MARKETING CAREER

Here are 16 product idea blueprints capable of launching your internet marketing career. By no means is this an exhaustive list; there are many more ideas that would work and I'm sure after you read through them, you'll start to get ideas of your own.

As you read through each one, you'll probably see some that are "just not for me." If that's the case, just skip it and go on to the next one. There's plenty to choose from, starting with the blueprint I modeled after to write this report. I completely changed the original idea, but the *seed* is still there. That's why I'm calling these *Radioactive Seeds*.

Enjoy!

**P.S.:** It's always a good idea to do a little research on the meaning of things before you jump in with both feet...

I foolishly and spontaneously named this report during a comic-bookish storm of creativity. I imagined a seed which had been bombarded with high doses of radiation causing a genetic mutation which resulted in a freakishly large and self-aware plant that goes on a destructive rampage throughout the city.

The basic premise was that even a small seed can grow into something gigantic.

Unfortunately, after about the 3rd update, I discovered "radioactive seeds" are testicular implants used to fight prostate cancer.

Live and learn.

Anyway... to make things easier and more convenient, I've started each blueprint at the top of a separate page.

## Radioactive Seed #1: "X-Ways To…" Report

With this idea you gather up a number of ways to do something internet marketing-related, then issue a report.

The report you're reading right now started out as an example of an "X-Ways To…" Report. I started out with a list of 16-ways to enter the internet marketing niche with a first product. It ultimately evolved into the report you're now reading.

It doesn't have to be 16-ways, it can be 10-ways… 7-ways… 5-ways or even only 3-ways as long as you're providing something valuable for your reader.

Examples would be:

*5 Simple Ways to Generate Fast Content*

*10 Unique Ways to Improve Crappy PLR Reports*

You could easily just spend an hour or two searching online for stuff to put into your report. Remember the basic concept: even though it's freely available on the internet doesn't mean it's not valuable. If you save someone several hours of search and evaluation time, it has value.

I particularly like the "X-Ways to…" reports as a first product idea because it's something anyone can do without too much knowledge on a subject. Create your report as you learn.

## Radioactive Seed #2: Summit Report

The idea behind this is simple: Attend a summit or conference related to internet marketing, take notes, then put them into a PDF report.

Something like this never occurred to me until I saw a WSO for the *2012 Traffic & Conversion Summit Notes* by Tim Castleman and Tanner Larsson.

What these guys did was attend the *2012 Traffic & Conversion Summit* put on by Ryan Deiss and Perry Belcher down in San Diego, then published a PDF report of the notes they took while listening to the presenters.

They reportedly sold over 2,000 copies starting at $7 each with the price increasing every sale. I think they did pretty well.

Of course, you'd have to attend the conference and take notes, but a lot of people do just that and come away with something they could sell and don't even know it!

There are whole businesses based on this one concept. Check out *My Note Taking Nerd*.

They attend summits and conferences, take notes, and then sell their *Nerd Reports* for $30 to $40... and, from what I've heard, they sell a *lot* of them.

Some of the conferences are quite pricey to attend (I recently saw one that was $2,000), so forking over $30 for a good report is a more reasonable option for people who can't afford to be there.

But, don't think it has to be a premium conference, either! People will pay money to save time. As long as there's value in your report, and you can articulate the value to your prospective customers, you'll have a good shot at success.

## Legal Ramifications

Before you run off and do one of these reports, do yourself a favor and actually get the permission of the event organizers/presenters before you proceed.

There's obviously going to be some copyrighted material involved and the last thing you want is a lawsuit. So, make sure you check out all the legal issues beforehand.

I'm not a lawyer and I sure don't want to give out any advice that will get you into trouble, so for this one, I have to insist you get permission in writing from event organizers / presenters, and then talk to an actual lawyer.

## Radioactive Seed #3: Fast-Article Writing Course

A lot of online marketers need to write articles, so this idea is usually pretty popular.

Look, I don't care if you've never written an article in your life; you can create a *How to Write a Fast Article* course. Here's why: nearly every course I've ever seen on writing fast articles follows this same advice:

1. **Research to find three or four main points for your topic**
2. **Break each main point down into 3 or 4 sub-points**
3. **Start writing using this article structure:**
   a. Tell them what you're going to tell them
   b. Tell them
   c. Tell them what you've told them
4. **Finished**

In your course, all you really have to do is come up with some innovative ways of doing fast research and then explain in detail how to use the above format.

It's really pretty simple. In order to show your customers how write a fast article, tell them to take each main point and sub-point then write a paragraph or two for each one. That will make up the bulk of their (b. Tell them) section. Then show them how to go back and write the (a. Tell them what you're going to tell them) and (c. Tell them what you've told them) sections based on what they wrote in the middle section.

For example, to write an article on the *Samsung Galaxy Note 8* smartphone, you'd show them how to structure it like this:

*In this article I'm going to show you why the Samsung Galaxy Note 8 is the greatest smartphone to come along in quite a while; I'm also going to tell you why the high price tag is nothing when you consider the state-of-the-art technology you'll get.* **[I'm telling you what I'm going to tell you].**

*First, let's look at the super large screen... blah, blah, blah... etc.* **[this would be the "tell them" section where you cover all the main points and sub-points and is the first section you should write].**

*So, when it comes to great smartphones, the Galaxy Note 8 hits on all cylinders. I've shown how the extra processing power is plenty to push the pixels for the extra large screen. I've also explained how the blah... blah... blah... etc.* **[tell them what you've told them].**

Of course, in your examples you'll be more detailed and complete than I was above, but you get the idea.

I really want to stress that the key to a successful Fast-Article Writing Course is showing how to do *fast research*. So, you've got your work cut out for you.

Come up with great ways to do that and your buyers

## WILLIAM MCCAMMENT

**will love you!**

## Radioactive Seed #4: Fast Product Creation Course

If you want to step it up a notch, use the previous seed as a guide and expand it into a *Fast Product Creation Course*. To create a fast product, you need to instruct your reader to include the following sections:

**INTRODUCTION**
**COPYRIGHT PAGE**
**STEP-BY-STEP "HOW-TO" SECTION**
**CONCLUSION**

They can add other sections as well, but the above four are pretty much mandatory. In your report, teach the reader to write the introduction and conclusion LAST based on what was taught in the "how-to" section.

The "how to" section should be structured in Step-by-Step format, like this:

**Step One: Do this...**
**Step Two: Do that...**
**ETC.**

Note that you don't have to literally call it, "Step One... Step Two..." etc. You just need to somewhat use that structured format. And, that applies to all the other sections as well.

In the original Radioactive Seeds report I didn't have

a section called, "Introduction." Instead, I changed the name to "Welcome!"

It's perfectly OK to do that sort of thing as long as you follow the basic format.

Teach your reader to fill-out each section using the fast-article writing system laid out in the previous seed.

You can fill-out your report with your best techniques for research, formatting a PDF, etc.

Like the previous seed, the key to this idea is to teach your readers *fast* product creation. Anything you can come up with to streamline the creation process will weigh heavily on the success of your product. So, you've got your work cut out for you double-time on this one. But, hopefully, I've sent you in the right direction.

## Radioactive Seed #5: Reference Guide

To create a reference guide you would go through an application or platform and briefly explain what each feature does.

For example, if I were going to create a reference guide for WordPress, I'd go into the WordPress dashboard for one of my sites and go down the left-hand sidebar and click on each tab one-by-one to explain each feature.

You don't need to explain everything in great detail—this is only a reference guide—a sentence or two is all you need. Maybe throw in a few screenshots.

You could actually go even simpler! How about a reference guide for WordPress that shows only the daily operation of a WordPress blog? You could sell it to warriors that build WordPress sites for offline businesses. They could give it to their clients so they don't have to go through teaching every client how to do the everyday tasks such as posting or updating. It's simple, but it's needed.

For your first product I suggest you keep your reference guide simple and cover only the basic features. You can always expand on it later for version 2.0 if you want.

While I'm on this subject: Somebody put together a simple reference guide that covers only the formatting aspects of Microsoft Word!

I'm sure I'm not the only one that would love to

format their PDFs without having to go through miles of extra explanation to get it done. I just want something that goes, "How to Add Page Numbers to your Document. Step One: do this... Step Two: do this... etc."

Find out the most popular formatting techniques for *Microsoft Word* and put together a PDF explaining each one in step-by-step format. I'd easily buy something like that *myself*.

And, don't forget the screenshots!

## Radioactive Seed #6: Research Pack

This can be extremely valuable to the right marketer. What you do is gather research on a popular niche like weight loss or golf and issue it as a report. But, instead of targeting the respective niches themselves, you target *the marketers* who are operating within those niches.

It's not really difficult because the research most marketers want is simple statistics. For example, if we were going to issue a research pack for the weight loss niche we would gather statistical answers to questions like the following:

What is the average success rate for dieters in general?

How many weight loss products does the average overweight person try in their lifetime?

What is the most weight a person can lose each day and still remain healthy?

A 3 to 7-page report filled with such statistics is all you really need – just make sure you pick a niche popular with online marketers.

Many marketers will buy this report and use the statistics in their sales letters and products. It saves them time from having to do the research on their own. And, it's absolutely necessary for some niches.

## Radioactive Seed #7: Simplified Process Video

With this you simply take a complicated internet marketing-related process and boil it down into a simple step-by-step video. For example, *How To Set-Up And Use An Autoresponder*.

A lot of people just don't want to go through the hassle of learning through trial and error. So, put together a video to help them out.

I think videos work better than PDFs for this one because customers can visually see what you're doing rather than trying to follow along with a written report. Also, videos are easier... just record the process as you're doing it and verbally explain each step.

Other examples would be:

*How To Set-Up and Start a Blog*

*How To Set-Up and Use Amazon S3*

Several years ago I was looking for an *Amazon S3* product to get me up to speed, but I had a real hard time finding it. Finally I found one by Wil Mattos. I don't remember what I paid for it, but it wasn't cheap—a lot more expensive than a typical WSO—but, I didn't care; I really needed it at the time and it was exactly what I was looking for.

Experienced marketers don't mind spending a few bucks on things like this; it's really only the unsuccessful and beginners that are always looking to figure everything out for themselves the long and hard way. Speed of learning is crucial when you're serious about business. Time is money.

If you know your subject, you can literally create a product like this in a matter of an hour or two. So, what are you waiting for?

## Radioactive Seed #8: List of Resources

Of all the ideas in this entire report, this has got to be the easiest. All we're doing is gathering a list of links to websites featuring internet marketing-related resources.

For example:

*250 Places to Get Royalty-Free Images*

*50 Places to Submit Your Site and Get it Indexed.*

Now, you actually have to put some effort into a report like this—don't just grab links and list them. Take some time to check out each and every link to make sure it isn't broken and has value. I've purchased these reports before and got irritated when a significant portion of the links were dead or went to a really bad resource.

I also suggest you put in at least a couple hours putting this list together and compiling an unusually large list if possible, otherwise you'll get a lot of, *Why would I buy this report when I could just look it up myself?*

People will *pay good money* to save the time and agony of finding good quality resources. So, spend enough time to make it valuable to them.

Also, remember to keep it current and updated so you can continue to resell it. There's a resource list of quality *Fiverr* vendors that has sold really well, and the people who use it buy the updated versions as they come out. It's almost like recurring income for the creator of that product.

## Radioactive Seed #9: Interview a Guru

You've probably heard of this one before: Interview a guru on a popular topic and sell the resulting MP3 or transcript. You can record a conversation over the phone or simply send him or her a series of questions to answer via email.

Maybe something like: *Insane Guru Spills the Beans About List-Building*

This was a popular idea a few years ago; however, if you've ever tried contacting a well-known guru to request an interview, you were likely either turned down or never received a reply at all.

Even though it's well-known, I'm including it here because it really is a great way to break into the internet marketing niche if you can get the interview.

Here's one way that might work, but you'll have to settle for building a list and not making money: Offer to give the guru *all* the money.

Don't bother trying to contact big-name gurus because they won't do it even if you offer them 100% of the profit... it's just not worth it to them.

I suggest you try to work something out with a newly-successful marketer on the Warrior Forum – they're a lot more likely to grant you an interview. You might even strike a 50-50 deal to split the profits with them.

Try to pick a topic they are known for such as list-building or traffic generation and pose a dozen or so questions directly related to that topic.

You can even take it to the next level by interviewing several marketers and putting together a grand collection of interviews. These sell pretty well at fairly high price-points—especially if you get some recognized talent involved.

I recently saw one of these interview collections being sold by someone I've never heard of, but the interviews featured some pretty big names (including Tony Robbins).

So, the point is, you can be a total nobody, but as long as you get truly qualified, knowledgeable people to interview, you can score big. And, remember, it doesn't have to be a big name like Tony Robbins; it just has to be someone credible with some desired knowledge and a successful track record.

## Radioactive Seed #10: PLR Report

Just in case you don't' know, PLR stands for *Private Label Rights*. What this means is you create a report in a popular niche and sell it with rights to let the buyer put his/her name on it and sell it as his/her own work. They can change it, add to it, break it up into articles, etc.

PLR is typically issued in PDF format but must also contain the original Word and/or plain text files. I recommend supplying both.

You can make a lot of money selling PLR, especially if it's high quality. Here's how…

A **good quality** PLR report should sell for a *minimum* of $25. You restrict sales to only about 100 or 200 copies at most to reduce market saturation (the fact is, most people that buy PLR will never use it so there really isn't any significant market saturation, but mention it anyway; it's a great selling point).

Let's say you create a good PLR report and put it on the Warrior Forum as a WSO. You limit it to 150 copies and sell it for $25 each. If you sell-out that's $3,750.

Now, even if you take 2-weeks to create such a report it means you could average two reports per month and bring in over $7,000 a month! Not bad.

Maybe I'm being over optimistic here, but even if you only sell $4,000 worth you're still making over a thousand a week.

Remember, I'm talking about really good quality PLR,

not the crap you find at mega-PLR websites... that stuff isn't worth using as toilet paper. Seriously.

Here's another idea: If you've tried any of the other report-type ideas in this section and it didn't quite work out, consider selling it as PLR. Maybe someone else can make it work. Heck! You've already got it completed; you may as well take another shot at generating some income from it.

## Radioactive Seed #11: Autoresponder Sequence

When marketers in various niches build an email list, they need to keep their subscribers happy by sending them valuable content. Why not create a sequence of emails they can use to do that?

Popular email sequences are things like a 5-part mini-course or 7-secrets to improve your golf swing.

These email sequences don't have to be very long, anywhere between 5 and 15 emails is good, but the longer the sequence, the more money you can charge.

Also, the content of each email only has to be around 4 or 5 paragraphs.

My suggestion is to shoot for sequences in the big niches such as weight loss or golf.

Issue a pack of 5 to 15 emails in plain text format and sell it as PLR for $7. I've paid $75 for a 365-day sequence in the health niche, so this idea is definitely scalable.

An offshoot of this would be to create a blog post sequence, but those generally extend much further in both content length and the number of posts, so take that into consideration before jumping into it.

## Radioactive Seed #12: Marketing Mindset

A lot of beginning marketers have trouble getting themselves to take action. If you can create a good report or video series that teaches them how to be more productive and take action it should sell fairly well.

It probably won't be a blockbuster though... after all, with this product, you'll be trying to sell to people that don't take action. ☺

The good news is that it's definitely an evergreen niche; marketers will need this type of thing until the end of time, so you can sell it for years.

Grab yourself a bunch of books on taking action, motivation and overcoming procrastination and suck out the best ideas to use in your report. Put your own special spin on it and you're ready to go.

Don't just sit there! Get motivated! ☺

## Radioactive Seed #13: Software/Web App Instruction

The idea behind this is to simply do a screencast video teaching people how to use a popular internet marketing application such as ClickFunnels or Google Analytics.

You don't need to show them every feature, just the basics to get them started.

Learning to use software or web apps can be a real pain when first starting out and seeing someone explain it on video can really help. A couple years ago I bought a video course on using PowerPoint. It wasn't cheap, but I'm happy I did because it shaved *days* off the time I would've spent trying to learn otherwise.

The most popular screencast application is Camtasia, but that will set you back about $300. A free alternative from the same company is Jing, but you are limited on the length of the videos.

Another screencast tool to check out is Screencast-O-Matic. You just go to their website and click the "Start Recording" button and it starts recording your screen. The basic version is free, but there's a premium version with more features.

I use the premium version ($15 a year) a lot... I even use it more than I use the $300 Camtasia which I also own and keep purchasing expensive upgrades (I don't know why... I must be the stupidest turnip off the truck).

Seriously, Screencast-O-Matic produces nice videos,

faster rendering time, smaller file sizes and the editing tools are much easier to learn.

I've also heard good things about ScreenFlow for Mac, but I'm a PC guy (at the moment), so I can't give an informed recommendation.

There are some other free options out there too if you do a Google search for "free screencast software" but I seriously doubt you'll do better than the free versions of Jing and Screencast-O-Matic (especially SOM).

## Radioactive Seed #14: Graphics Pack

Sales page graphics sell pretty well on the Warrior Forum, so it can be a great way to break into the Online Marketing niche. You don't even have to create the graphics yourself, simply hire a graphic designer to do it for you.

You'll want to supply Headers, Banners, Check Marks, Testimonial Boxes, etc. Check the WSO section of the Warrior Forum to see what I'm talking about—there's always a few of these graphics packs being sold. If you see something you like, hire a graphics designer and show it to him or her and say you'd like your own original version of that. Simple.

You'll want to set it up so you can give your customers PNG, JPG and original Photoshop files.

This idea can cost a bit upfront if you don't create the graphics yourself—maybe $300 or so to hire someone—but, like I said, it's a great way to get started in the Online Marketing niche.

If you do hire someone, make sure to have them create a nice header graphic for your WSO or sales page as well.

There are several PLR graphics packages out there, also. I wouldn't just repackage one of those, but you can purchase a PLR license and add it to yours to increase the number of graphic elements. Just a thought.

## Radioactive Seed #15 "What I found out..." Report

This idea involves taking a larger work (or several works), focusing on one important aspect, adding to it, and then boiling it down into an informative report.

It is critical that you take on the role of "reporter" rather than "expert" for this seed unless you really do have some expertise in the topic. That way, you don't look like you're overstepping your bounds trying to look more qualified than you really are. It's best to be as honest as possible and clarify that you are gathering information and not basing it on personal experience.

The first thing you'll need to do is find a popular book—or, better yet, several books—covering some important aspect of internet marketing or making money online.

For example, I'm looking at a great SEO book called, *SEO for 2013: Search Engine Optimization Made Easy*. Yes, it's an older book from 2013, but, I had it sitting here handy, and for the purposes of this explanation, it will do. However, you might want to find something more up-to-date (I don't plan on buying the latest version, I rarely mess around with my own SEO anymore. Also, a quick check at Amazon reveals the authors left off at 2014, so it appears you *can't* get an up-to-date version anyway).

The book covers just about every aspect of SEO from submitting your site to Google, to what to do if you've been banned by the search engines.

One section covers professional SEO services and

what to look for when hiring one. You could take that section, extract the most important points, arrange them into a step-by-step format and turn it into a *What I Found Out About Hiring an SEO Service Without Getting Ripped Off* report.

Now, we're not talking about plagiarism here, we're only taking short notes to use as a road map for our step-by-step report.

We're also going to expand on what is covered in the book. For instance, the section on hiring an SEO service only lists one place to find such a service: theirs.

Adding a list of resources to find a reputable SEO service would be something I'd definitely add. You'd have to get on the Warrior Forum and research warriors offering SEO services with lots of positive feedback, but that's easy enough to do.

Remember, we aren't rewriting the whole book, just an important section which we can use as a guide in creating a saleable report. I'm sure if you went to your local *Barnes & Noble* bookstore, you could find a few books with great ideas.

When I come up with these types of reports, I usually start with the title and it always starts like this:

"What I found out about..."

*What I Found Out About Ad Retargeting*

*What I Found Out About Article Marketing*

The cool thing is *you don't have to have any real expertise* if you title it like this because you are only claiming to reveal *what you found out*. Pure genius!

The possibilities are endless.

## Radioactive Seed #16: Video Review Packages

Here's a great way to build a list of buyers with the potential to buy from you again and again: What you do is pick the top five ClickBank products in any popular niche. Use screen capture software such as Camtasia to record yourself buying and reviewing each product, then sell the rights to the videos as a WSO for affiliate marketers to use on their sites.

The drawback is that it's going to cost you money upfront to buy the products unless you're able to swing a "Review Copy" deal, but what a great way to get started building a list of buyers that need someone to supply and recommend future marketing products!

And, think about this... after you sell them your review videos, you'll also have these clients on a list where you can promote (through your affiliate link) things like WordPress themes, lead-generation products, graphics packs, etc.

SNEAKY BONUS TRICK: If you already sell your own niche product on ClickBank, make sure you include a review of that one as well! ☺

# OFFERING SERVICES

## Article Writing Service

I couldn't include this in the seeds because it's a 100% service oriented project, but if you use the article writing format I suggested in the *Fast-Article Writing Course* seed, you have a good shot to make this work.

Writing articles is always in demand. The biggest drawback is that a lot of people offer this service and you'll have to be pretty fast at pumping them out in order to compete. Still, it's a great way to get started in the internet marketing niche as long as you're a decent writer and can provide some good sample articles.

Speed is the key... if you can research and write a 400-word article in ten minutes or less then you have a shot. I'm serious. You've got to be insanely quick in order to keep your prices down.

If I were going to do this I'd definitely look into using voice recognition software such as *Dragon Naturally Speaking*. It could be the edge you need to make this work.

Service oriented WSOs aren't going to propel you into the IM world at alarming speed until people get to know who you are and what you can do for them, so you might want to choose something else in this report, but it's something to think about if you're skilled.

## Sales Video Service

Here's another service oriented idea you can do that doesn't require so much high speed work. You'll need to create a few samples of your work in order to let potential customers know you are capable, but if you speak clear, understandable English, there's definitely a need for something like this.

You can use something like PowerPoint to create sales videos for marketers. The kind that feature only text with someone (you) reading the text as it appears on the screen. I'm sure you've seen what I'm referring to here.

It's pretty common knowledge that these videos convert better than traditional sales letters in a lot of cases, and a lot of people have no clue how to use PowerPoint. Also, if English is their second language they'll really appreciate your service creating these videos for them.

Offer to create a sales video based on their sales letter... it could not be easier! All you do is use the text in their sales letter as the basis for your sales video. You might have to tweak it a bit to make it work, but it should be pretty easy.

Be sure to create one of these for yourself selling your video sales service to show what you can do and put it in your WSO thread or on your sales page.

# PIGGYBACKING

Here's a concept that is almost guaranteed to make some sales. What you do is build upon a popular product scheme currently bombarding the Warrior Forum's WSO section.

Every once in a while a recurring idea hits the Warrior Forum and everyone jumps on it every which way from Sunday. Recently, that was whiteboard-style video sales letter software. Everyone and their monkey trainer put out one of these software packages.

Anyway, several of these packages became *WSO of the day* and sold by the truckload. The problem with these packages, though, is there's only so many graphics included and pretty soon everyone's sales videos have the same look.

They're nice looking videos, but people want individuality. So, a few smart entrepreneurs *piggybacked* on the success of the hot new software trend and created graphics packs specifically for these applications!

Keep in mind that they didn't have to include any software—everyone already owned the necessary software—all they had to do was offer graphics that would work with the software.

How easy is that? Just commission someone to create a bunch of whiteboard-style sales graphics and sell to the hot new market. A couple of these stand-alone graphics packages were popular enough to be featured on JVZoo and WarriorPlus as daily picks. They sold a ton.

So, the whole idea behind piggybacking is to simply jump on an already hot trend and create a co-product that fits.

Try to figure out what all the people buying on such a trend are going to need and supply a co-product.

Remember, you don't have to create the product yourself; you can farm it out to an outsourcer if necessary. Just be quick about it before the trend dies down.

# DOING YOUR FIRST WSO

B ack in 2013 when I first wrote Radioactive Seeds and it was offered as a PDF eBook, the Warrior Forum was still under the same management and ownership as it was when I first became a member in 2007.

It was a lot easier to use whatever payment processor you wanted and I've always used JVZoo.

After doing a final check on what's going on over there at Warrior Forum these days, if you've never done a WSO before, I've concluded it would just be so much easier to use their in-house payment processor, Warrior Payments.

The main reason is it's just too inconvenient now to use JVZoo or Warrior+.

Besides, it's as simple as watching the nifty walkthrough video they have that explains every single detail.

The only caveat I have is that I've never personally used Warrior Payments so I can't give you a first-hand explanation of anything. However, after watching the training video, it doesn't look like it's going to be much trouble.

Warrior Payments eliminates what I think is the biggest drawback to using a 3rd party payment processor like JVZoo: The ability to preview your WSO before it goes live.

Of course, if you're a War Room Member you get access to the Test Forum, but that's an extra $97 per year.

Another plus is that it's super easy to set everything up. When I first watched the video I did one of those "I could have had a V8" head slaps.

Anyway, everything you'll need to know to setup a WSO using Warrior Payments can easily be found by doing a search on YouTube for "how to create a product to sell on Warrior Payments."

Look for the video put out by Warrior Forum.

Of course, once you've done a few WSOs with Warrior Payments, you could definitely look into other payment processors.

## Protected Downloads

Before you get too far along with your WSO, you're going to want to consider how you'll deliver your digital product. You want to make sure only paying customers can get a hold of it.

All of the major payment processors like Warrior Payments, JVZoo or Warrior+ have the option to upload your (128mb or less) product directly with them.

In other words, you can just create your sales page on Warrior Forum and use one of those payment processors for the product delivery. You don't even have to have your own website.

This is definitely the easiest and recommended option.

The other option is to use a protected *Thank You* page on your own web site to deliver the product.

This is serious business if you don't have membership software in place. However, most membership software companies offer tutorials on how to protect downloads from a *Thank You* page.

There are several membership plugins for WordPress that have built-in payment processor compatibility, but at the time I'm writing this, I haven't tested any of them aside from InstaMember and MemberSonic.

Both are pretty good... I especially liked InstaMember while I was using it, but after I began using ClickFunnels for almost everything I haven't kept up on how well it performs these days. I suspect it's still pretty good (and, at the time of this writing, the few sites I still have it running on still receive updates and I haven't had any recent issues).

## Posting Your First WSO

Once you're all set up and written your sales letter, it's a good idea to preview what your WSO will look like to the public. If you're satisfied and everything looks good, go ahead and submit the order.

The way they run things now is that you'll have to pay for your WSO before the Warrior Forum moderators put it through the approval process. Also, I don't think there are any refunds beyond this point, so be careful.

Once you pay and submit your WSO it will have to go

through an approval process before you can go any further. Once it's approved, you'll receive a private message indicating you've been approved along with instructions on how to make your WSO visible.

That's all there is to it! You've just set up and submitted your first WSO! All that's left now is to make sales. Good luck!

# JUMPSTARTING YOUR WSO

One of the most important things I can teach you about WSO's is that their success is highly fueled by testimonials. People want some reassurance that what they're about to buy isn't junk. There's so many lousy WSO's out there these days that the forum is pretty jaded and skeptical.

You can have a killer sales page and still not make significant sales until some encouraging testimonials start rolling in. But, since this is your first WSO and you haven't made any sales yet, how do you go about getting some?

A lot of Warriors start out by giving away review copies. They'll post their WSO with a message at the top of the sales page (or, even in the listing text) that says, "REVIEW COPIES AVAILABLE." Then they get a barrage of requests from mostly inexperienced Warriors trying to get a free WSO.

Sometimes this works out but more often than not the biggest share of people reviewing the WSO have only one or two posts in their post count and their "join date" is the current year. In other words, they lack credibility and people immediately jump to the conclusion the account was created for the sole purpose of leaving a review.

I think a much better idea is to go looking for credible people to give you testimonials before you even launch your WSO. There are a few good ways to go about this. One way is to post an ad in the classified section of the Warrior Forum. It's going to cost you $20, but it could get you some good reviews pretty quickly.

I like this method because you can list minimum requirements for receiving a review copy such as the reviewer has to have at least 25 posts and have been a member of the forum for at least two years.

In addition, you can have them post the review right there in the classified section and "review" their review. If it's a good one, you can have them repost it to your WSO page, if it's not so good, leave it alone.

The other way to get credible reviews is to go looking for people that posted good reviews on other WSOs and send them a private message to see if they'd be interested in reviewing your product. If they say OK then send them a copy and let them post the review to your WSO.

You'll save $20 this way, but you also run the risk associated with not getting a chance to see it before it goes live on your WSO. I suppose you could ask them to let you see it first, but doing that sort of thing gets to be a hassle for the reviewer and they might just ignore you or, worse, give you a bad review because you're a pest.

Another idea is to go looking in the main internet marketing discussion forum for people asking questions that could be answered by your WSO. Send them a private message and tell them you think your product would help them and you'll send them a review copy for free.

However, make sure you tell them a review is optional because these types of people tend to feel pressure and don't do such a good job of reviewing your product. If you tell them it's optional they seem to loosen up and most times give a decent review.

If you do get a bad review the first thing you should do is read it and figure out if the reviewer has a point. If he or she does, maybe you should update your product to correct the problem.

If the bad review is completely off-base, then you can report it and get it removed.

Unfortunately, you'll see a few people—for whatever reason—who have a great need to destroy the reputation of others (usually, it's due to their inability to cope with their microscopic genitalia). If they are overly abusive, simply report the post and get it removed. Don't try and battle with these angry little trolls—it's too much of a distraction for those deciding whether to buy your product.

# HOW TO BURY MEDIOCRE REVIEWS AND UNCOMFORTABLE QUESTIONS

Sometimes you'll get reviews that aren't necessarily bad but don't really help to sell your product. Also, you might get some questions about you or your product that detract from its selling points.

For example, even though you're selling a product that requires no proof, a lot of times someone will jump in and ask a credibility question such as, "How many successful WSOs have you run?"

Now, even though you have nothing to prove, you'd still like this question to go away because it focuses on your inexperience.

The first piece of advice I'd like to give you is, *don't panic*. Instead, try to turn it into an opportunity to sell more products. It might take a bit of ingenious salesmanship on your part, but it can be done.

Here's what I did when I got that *exact* question for my first WSO... the first version of Radioactive Seeds.

The very first comment I got was, "How many successful WSOs have you run?"

Now, the correct answer, of course, was, "Zero."

But, if I had answered it like that I'm sure it would have affected sales because it focused too much on my inexperience at the time in the "make money online" niche and people are so skeptical of newbie WSOs.

So, after the initial panic wore off I set out to turn it into a positive—remember, this was my very first comment on my very first WSO sales page and a lot was riding on my answer. Here's how I answered it:

**Member Question:** *How many successful WSO's have you run?*

**My Response:** *Thanks for the question. This is my FIRST WSO. So, the first thing I'd like to say is: If I can do it YOU can do it. But, I'm not just showing you how to do a WSO—there's a zillion other WSOs out there you can find for that—I'm showing you how someone with no past history or proof of income can legitimately break into the internet marketing niche with their VERY FIRST product.*

*You can't sell a Make Money Online product if you have no practical experience behind it. My WSO shows you how to get around this barrier and create VALUABLE products for this niche. I give you 16-examples of products that have proven to be successful for their creators. None of them require past history or proof of income to work.*

*I give you the main concept behind all of these products and, yes, I even used it to create THIS VERY WSO.* ☺

I tried to answer it in a way that would not only quench

concerns for anyone else wondering the same thing, but also use my answer to *sell more products*!

Notice too, I didn't run away from the fact it was my first WSO, I took it head-on by emphasizing it with capital letters.

The last thing you want to do is get all defensive or evasive. What you can't hide, feature.

Have enough confidence in yourself and your abilities to put it all out there and make the case why they should listen to you.

If you give it some thought, you can turn just about any question into a sales boost. It might take some imagination and ingenuity on your part, but you can do it. Take your time, and think it out.

But, I have one more trick up my sleeve for reducing the blow of such questions and mediocre reviews: *push it down the page.*

When you get uncomfortable questions and mediocre reviews it would be nice to bury them further down the page and let the better reviews come first.

But, you have no control over who's post shows up first, right? It's on a first-come-first-served basis.

If the first response on your WSO comes from a vindictive troll, it's going to be the first thing everyone sees (unless it's so bad you have it removed by the moderators).

Pretty scary, huh?

Well, not really, because there's an easy way to wrestle control over all this.

The trick is to post a "Reserved for FAQs" comment immediately after your WSO goes live.

What this does is reserve the first comment for yourself so you can control what reviews visitors see first.

You should genuinely use this slot to field frequently asked questions, but the more valuable reason—for you—is to post quotes in excerpt form from your best reviews.

As good reviews come in, quote them in there just underneath the FAQ's, like this:

---

**Reserved for FAQ's**

Q: Are there any OTO's?

A: Nope.

**Here are excerpts from some of the top reviews:**

Quote:

Originally posted by DJX71>

*I'll get straight to it – this WSO offers lots of value for ANYONE (newbie or not), and currently is massively underpriced.*

---

And, then, just keep putting the best quotes from the best reviews you got underneath that one.

You can even grab several different quotes out of the same reviews and sprinkle them throughout that first slot. Just don't go overboard.

Anyway... That's a good technique to put your best reviews at the top of the page. It's always smart to give a good first impression.

If you did get a few bad reviews, this is a great way to tire the reader out before they get to them.

# THIS IS ONLY THE TIP OF THE ICEBERG

When you get right down to it, the product blueprints I introduced in this section are just the tip of the iceberg. The key advice and real value boils down to creating a product that satisfies the concept I discussed at the beginning:

*You <u>can't</u> legitimately show them how to make money, but you <u>can</u> help them to save money or be more efficient.*

Follow this one simple rule and you can create a whole series of products to sell to your list until you come up with a real, battle-tested money making system you can legitimately sell with all the proof-of-income screenshots and stories of overnight success.

And, so, this concludes the Radioactive Seeds section. I hope I was able to get your juices flowing for jumping into the "make money online" niche.

I know this isn't really for everyone, but if nothing

else, I hope you at least enjoyed it and maybe learned a thing or two.

# WELCOME TO THE MATRIX

Before you went through this book you might have thought things like giving away 150% commissions or spending $8 on advertising to sell a $7 eBook were crazy.

But, now that you've peeked into the *Online Money Matrix* and fully understand concepts like *Customer Lifetime Value*, do you still think so?

I don't think you do. Your eyes are open now. You have the ability to see the invisible.

I believe the lessons in this book will make the difference between making a few bucks online and having a full-blown internet marketing business.

I also believe if you want to be ultra-successful in the online marketing game there is no other way than to learn this stuff. The good news is that you have it here for easy reference any time you need to refresh your knowledge.

I know the math can get tedious and confusing at times, but it's not like you have to do it all day long; once you get your monthly income plan together all you have to do is implement it.

After you get good at it, it's kind of fun to sit down and map out a plan. Each time you create a new product you'll be able to add it into your income strategy and it will give you additional money-making scenarios to explore.

By reading this book you have learned what perhaps only one-in-a-thousand online marketers understand about the science of positive cash flow.

Create new products, build new sales-funnels, experiment and test.

Help people.

It took me nearly 20-years of trial-and-error online to fully get the gist of what I've taught you in this book. Trust me when I say there's some powerful stuff in here. It can change your whole perspective on online marketing and make an incredible impact on your career.

I hope you feel you've learned a thing or two and that the whole experience was at least a little bit entertaining.

See you next time!

**William McCamment**
DigitalProgressReport.com

## ABOUT THE AUTHOR

William McCamment is a writer, online marketing coach, business consultant and product creator who's been involved with online marketing and sales since 1995. He currently lives amongst the vineyards of Temecula, California with his wife Rachel and daughter Emily.

www.ingramcontent.com/pod-product-compliance
Lightning Source LLC
Chambersburg PA
CBHW020651220526
45464CB00001B/395